# TO STAY A BELIEVER

# TO STAY A BELIEVER

## the challenge to Christians in the age of technology

**Desmond O'Donnell OMI**

TWENTY-THIRD PUBLICATIONS
Mystic, Connecticut

North American Edition 1990

Twenty-Third Publications
P.O. Box 180
185 Willow Street
Mystic, CT 06355
(203) 536-2611



Simutaneously published in Ireland by The Columba Press, 93, The Rise, Mount Merrion, Blackrock, County Dublin.

ISBN 0-89622-462-7
Library of Congress Catalog Number 90-71271

# Preface

Each year, SEDOS, which represents the major Religious Orders in Rome, holds a study session on a subject of common interest and import. In 1988 they chose 'Modernity, Secularisation and Faith,' because they all experience increasing difficulty in proclaiming the Gospel to the modern world. I was privileged to address them on this subject and was asked thereafter to write something on it for the average Christian. This book is the result. It is intended for adults who feel the need to look at their changing experience of God today.

In most countries, there is growing discomfort among sincere Christians in reconciling their experience of the modern world with faith as they have known it. The drop in religious practice may or may not be connected to this questioning. The overall phenomenon is called 'secularisation'; the reality however is too varied and complex for this older word. The one common feature is this: as an unprecedented avalanche of information permeates people's lives through technology, it appears that faith and religious behaviour are losing ground. In this book I try to address the problem as simply as the subject will allow, with constant applications to everyday human experience.

Some of the ideas, concepts and conclusions of this book, especially in the first Part, may appear fairly intense and difficult to assimilate at the beginning. In order to help the first-time reader, I have supplied a set of three 'True or False' statements for each chapter which I hope might help you in reviewing your personal reading of each chapter in turn. You will find these grouped at the end of each Part of the book, along with some questions for group discussion.

One of the points made in Part Five is that Christians today really need the support of small groups of other believers. I believe that the best way to use this book would be in the context of a small group of fellow-believers, reading the book at the same time and meeting now and again to share and discuss it. To that end, I have supplied a set of questions for group discussion of each chapter. You may not go through each one of these questions in detail. You may decide, for example, to meet five times with your group, covering a full part of the book in each of the five discussions. Or you may decide to take two chapters per meeting and meet seven times.

In other words, adapt and use the book to suit your own arrangements and circumstances.

The best way to benefit from the book is to take it part by part or chapter by chapter with a small group of friends where, through sharing and discussion, learning best takes place.

I dedicate it to my parents through whom God founded and firmed my faith in a comparatively unchanging world, and to my friends who now help me find a tolerable sense of place and permanency in an ever-changing one.

# Contents

# TO STAY A BELIEVER

# *Part One*
# The World Now

Chapter 1:
Technology and change

Chapter 2:
How technology affects our lives

Chapter 3:
How technology affects religion and faith

# Chapter 1: Technology and change

*Introduction*

In a book on faith, you may be surprised to find only a brief reference to faith in this first section. The reason for this is that it is necessary to understand your own experience, before you can understand your experience of God. Your experience is that of a person living in a world of rapid change, brought about mainly by technology. This has a profound influence on faith.

> Your experience is that of a person living in a world of rapid change, brought about mainly by technology.

Change has always been part of the human experience but it has never come as quickly or as intensely as it has in the last fifty years. Nor is there any indication that it is going to slow down. Information travels faster, people move more often, and inventions – from kitchen mod-cons to complicated weaponry – follow one another with surprising speed.

If the last 50,000 years were divided into lifespans of 62 years, there would have been 800 such lifespans. 650 of these were spent in caves; only in the last 70 lifespans has communication by writing from one lifespan to the next been possible, and only during the last 6 have most people seen a printed word. Electricity came in the last 2 lifespans and most of the material goods we use came within the present lifespan.

Many of us remember the discovery of plastics in the 40s, of transistors in the 50s, of microtransistors in the 60s, and all adults among us have seen the first computers. Now in the 90s we all take genetic engineering for granted. And none of this – moving from cave to condominiums, from stone hatchets to sophisticated rocketry, from candles to coloured neon and from inter-village to inter-continental air transport – is just 'out there.' We know that it is affecting us; at least we know its benefits and suspect its less helpful contributions to human living.

Because the effects of change upon each of us are deep and far-reaching, we must be aware of them and think about them. We must carefully consider the effects of rapid change on our family life and our relationships. Change can undermine the very meaning of our lives and of our faith, even if unconsciously.

### *Change and Awareness*

Let us reflect on some of the more obvious changes which affect and challenge us. Despite the comparative ease of travel today, many people feel alone and lonely. Most of us were born into a town, a neighbourhood, or at least into a web of family relationships, which gave a comfortable feeling of belonging, even if it limited our privacy. Now many feel less neighbourliness and some feel painfully isolated from adequate human support.

Maybe we are fulfilling our shallow needs and forgetting our deeper ones.

Life was once a lot more pleasant in some ways because it was predictable and there seemed to be less competition. But even the near future seems unclear now, while local and intergroup conflict is never far away.

Work hours have become shorter, and some would say more human, but it is not clear that we are enjoying the leisure which this should bring us. The advertisements help us to find what we need but maybe we are fulfilling our shallow needs and forgetting our deeper ones; pleasure easily takes the place of deep enjoyment.

And yet, it does not seem that we can go back; we cannot stop the world and get off. Nor is it clear that individuals – as distinct from groups – can influence the speed of change. But we can certainly increase our awareness, and control our response, if we take the trouble to understand what is happening. This understanding begins when we see how technology (broadly, modern scientific inventions) has changed our experience of life.

*Understanding Technology*

The story of Adam and Eve reminds us that the human person has always sought more knowledge, while the libraries and data-banks of the world confirm it. Until comparatively recently in history, this knowledge remained in libraries and in centres of academic learning. Now it is being *dynamically transferred into technology* and, from there, into the lives of people everywhere. For example, the knowledge of how sound travels was of academic interest until it was transferred into the technology we call a telephone.

Other pieces of technology include cars, computers, airconditioners and aeroplanes, factory farming and FAX, radio, TV, and video, hairdryers, electric blankets, and microwaves. Each of these is affecting the human experience and apparently changing it in some ways all the time. Genetic engineering is perhaps the most dramatic. Chemistry gave us plastics; physics gave us computers; the biotechnologies promise us a 'new' person through defeat of diseases by the manipulation of the genetic code.

In most developed countries, bigness (the supermarket for instance) and efficiency (the telephone etc.) have made life easier in many ways, but the quality of life is not always and obviously improved.

Bigness and efficiency have made life easier in many ways, but the quality of life is not always improved.

Technology affects the human experience:

*Ecologically*, by controlling pests but damaging the ozone layer;

*Economically*, by facilitating trade but causing unemployment;

*Politically*, by diffusing information but centralising power;

*Culturally*, by changing unjust traditions but undermining meaningful symbol systems;

*Genetically*, by curing pre–natal defects but experimenting with human embryos;

*Religiously*, by explaining nature scientifically but causing an apparent withdrawal of God in people's experience.

In the past thirty years, we have seen more technological change than in all recorded history. It took 112 years for photography to go from discovery to commercial product; 56 years for the telephone; 35 years for radio; 15 for radar; 12 for television; but only 6 for the atomic bomb to become an operational reality, and only 5 for transistors to find their way from the laboratory to the market. Nowadays, a product can be invented, produced, packaged, marketed, and even bypassed by another similar invention, very quickly. However, before each invention has become obsolete, it has touched the human experience and changed it in some way.

Let us reflect for a while on the nature of technology itself. I suggest that you pause to think about each paragraph for a moment after reading it.

*Morally Neutral*

Technology is morally neutral; in itself, it is neither good nor evil. A helicopter can bring food to a starving village or can be used to bomb it; a telephone message can commence a lifelong friendship or plan a murder, and the bio-technologies can help childless couples, or kill an unborn baby. Technology usually demands that we know the cost of everything but the value of nothing, because values are not in its vocabulary.

Technology demands that we know the cost of everything but the value of nothing, because values are not in its vocabulary.

*Present everywhere*

As it expands into all countries and cultures, technology seems to be a culture of its own and tends to reduce all other cultures to its own image and likeness. Uncomplicated people, who dress with little but a lap-lap, now wear walkmans; obscure villages have instant communication through the transistor – with instant challenge to their ways of life. Systems like communism, successfully closed until recently, were questioned as the youth went disco-dancing and listened eagerly to foreign newscasts in their own language. Not only do the new media bring the news everywhere simultaneously, but they enable people to be 'present' everywhere as well, so that millions could say that they 'saw' the Berlin Wall fall – and almost danced with those coming through it!

*Self-propelling*

Technology appears to have its own momentum; it is self-propelled as the news media move information almost instantly. Scientists can compare and combine their discoveries and their inventions by visiting one another quickly, or communicating instantly by FAX. Each new invention can only be replaced by an improved one; it cannot be uninvented. Satisfying needs can create more needs, and technology does not favour slowing down or stopping this process.

*Addictive*

Because most modern inventions appeal to our desire for instancy, efficiency, comfort and control, they sell themselves; they are almost addictive, almost irresistible. The 'new' model is always 'better.' The passage from recognising that a new piece of technology might be *superfluous* in my life, to feeling its *attractiveness*, to thinking that it might be *useful*, to the conviction of its *necessity* and to the final step of feeling it is *indispensable*, is a very smooth one.

*Useful*

Technology says 'I am useful' and it usually is. In general, technology responds to immediate and measurable needs; it is functional. It is not concerned about higher manifestations of human life, like truth, beauty, nobility, loyalty or faith, since these cannot be measured in functional terms. This is why the changes being brought about by technology may be more a moral challenge than a faith one. Increasingly people are also asking just how useful new developments are – distinguishing between short-term and long-term usefulness.

*Directionless*

Technology thrives on the word *progress*, a high quality of which it often delivers, but it is not in the business of defining what is meant by 'progress.' For example, increased urbanisation, facilitated by technology, has not always led to true human progress.

The technological revolution knows what it is about to do, but it might not know what it is about.

*Unpredictable*

Technology encourages so much that is good – like information-openness, better communication, mutual respect among the various branches of learning – but in itself it is unpredictable.

Because it is more or less mindless, it does not know where it is going. It cannot foresee any future beyond the current invention. Its only limits are the ever-receding horizons of the designers' imaginations.

*Centralising*

One of the most interesting and serious qualities of technology is that it helps people to come together in large cities, thus increasing efficiency and employment in some cases, but causing pollution and unemployment in others. More seriously, it enables the centralisation of money and of power. For example, with modern weapons and fast communications, a thousand people can control a million. Again, with modern technology, individuals who have money can make more money much faster, and so technology contributes to increasing the gap between rich and poor. 'Merchants are replacing warriors as the main actors on the world stage.' (TIME magazine, 7.5.90)

*Widening Choice*

When the supermarket began to eliminate the corner shop, people's choice of material goods increased, even if the supermarkets can gradually capture, control and raise the cost of most things. Urban planners are faced with choices and decisions which may last a long time, and scientists working on the DNA have a constant demand for deep decisions also. Technology has moved much of life from fate to choice, and it very often calls for fairly instant choice too.

*In Summary*

'The process of technological progress is irreversible. This is a fact which we must recognise without indulging in useless regrets. Rather, the believer is grateful to God who has given humankind not only the ability, but also the responsibility, of developing the resources of creation. The activities associated with high technology are also part of ***human*** work and can therefore be vested with the same *dignity.*'

– *Pope John Paul*
to workers in high-tech factories at Ivrea, Italy, 19.3.90

## Reviewing Chapter One

Was there anything in this chapter to which you could immediately relate from your own experience?
Were there any new ideas which you found puzzling or worrisome?
Did you find in this chapter anything of benefit to you in your particular role as a Christian?
*You may find it helpful to make a note of any thoughts from this chapter which you would like to remember.*

## Questions for discussion in your group

1. How does technology (telephone, TV, fridge, computer, etc.) touch on your life at home, at work, in your hours of leisure?
2. Discuss ways in which technology is addictive in your life.
3. It is suggested that those living in a technological age are discouraged from looking for the deeper things in life. What do you think these deeper needs are, and are you, personally, discouraged from seeking them?

# Chapter 2:
# How technology affects our lives

Many thinkers are of the opinion that humankind is now at a significant hinge in its history; they are already talking about the post-technology or post-modern era. The changes brought about by the technological revolution, and the speed at which they have come and continue to come, demands an individual and collective response. Modernity – the marriage of an unprecedented flow of knowledge and an ever advancing technology – can contribute to a better world for all of us, or can dehumanise and even destroy us very suddenly. We must decide which it will be.

Modernity can contribute to a better world for all of us, or can dehumanise and even destroy us. We must decide which it will be.

At first, technology *facilitated* what was already being done, as tools increased precision and production. Then it began to *transform* what was already being done, as when transport moved into steam, electricity and nuclear power. Now it seems to be almost *creative*, as plant, animal and human life are being manipulated at their very centre. This movement from being facilitative, to being transformative, to being almost creative, calls for deep awareness by every responsible person.

*Ecology*

Pope John Paul II said, at New Year 1990, 'Certain elements of today's ecological crisis reveal its moral character. First among these is the indiscriminate application of advances in science and technology. Many recent discoveries have brought undeniable benefits to humanity. Indeed, they demonstrate the nobility of the human vocation to participate responsibly in God's creative action in the world. Unfortunately, it is now clear that the application of these discoveries in the fields of industry and agriculture have produced harmful long-term effects. This has led to the painful realisation that we cannot interfere in one area of the ecosystem without paying due attention both to the consequences of such interference in other areas and to the well-being of future generations.'

*The Family*

Family members can travel to visit one another more easily than before and the telephone can be a great opportunity to 'meet' more often. All, thanks to technology. But it is the same technology which leads to redundancy, demands harder work, keeps parents away from children they love, insists on early retirement and puts students under great pressure. Tension and tiredness seem to be by-products of modern life for most people, and this in turn has profound effects on how we relate to one another – another challenge.

Tension and tiredness seem to be by-products of modern life.

*The Electronic Media*

Few things indicate the presence of the technological revolution as clearly as the media of communication – print, radio, TV and video. So much about these is helpful – they educate, relax and amuse us. Again, they are morally neutral, but can serve immoral ends, depending on how they are used. One of the obvious results is that they set up a dependency on them; they steal our time. Many programmes make us think, but overall the media do not encourage or even allow us to reflect. Packaged messages are given, and momentary stimulation appears to be the purpose of most programmes and even of many items of 'news.'

However, the major influence of the media is not in the new products they promote nor in the new behaviour which they show and which might be imitated. Their major influence is on how we relate to each other as people. People are naturally separated in various ways, for example, in homes (parents from children), in offices (bosses from employees), in a street (house from house), country from country (rich from poor), or group from group (the sexes). Imagine that all these separations were permanently removed, so that most of other people's activities were visible to all. Students would see teachers argued down by their own children, employees would see their bosses manipulated by their spouses, voters would see their politicians drink too much, parishioners would see the sins of their priests and children would see all of their parents' actions. What a change in behaviour and self-image this would bring to each of us! But this is already taking place, as the media enable people to see the private lives of others, either directly or in replay or simulation.

Because of this, the images we have of others are fractured and frequently re-made by the media, or by our own judgement of what we see or hear. Our attitudes towards others then change and the same is true in reverse: other people's images of us change, and as a consequence, so does their behaviour towards us. It is then inevitable that our own image of ourselves, our sense of identity, undergoes a change as well. Because of the media, presidents, politicians and priests, homosexuals, hot-gospellers and handicapped people – indeed, all of us in some way – have their images and sense of identity loosened up or dismantled.

So, the electronic media call for a stance, a response and a discipline, unless we are willing to be passively moulded by them.

*Travel*

Technology gives us much with which to fill our time – notably travel to show us the world, and gadgets to keep us busy. There is also less time for meaningful communication among family members and friends. Perhaps we see and work with more people, but do we touch them, with time to pass on care and concern or the pleasant and painful moments we all like to share? Once, we knew our neighbours and maybe their parents; now, because of

> Distrust is never far away in modern life.

fast mobility, we often do not know who lives next door. Distrust is never far away in modern life.

*Education*

Teachers are doing their best to prepare children for the future and technology can provide an aid as helpful as the overhead projector. But the same technology has made the future of our children very unclear. The future is now equally full of promise and of threat, as human survival is being trusted more to technological advances than to civic virtue. Many educationalists say that we can educate children today only with values for choice, as the unknown futures race into their lives. And two important childhood experiences – fantasy and freedom to play – are being pressured out by hectic educational programmes.

*Marriage*

Few wives and mothers are not grateful to technology for a dishwasher, a hairdryer, a fridge and a microwave oven. It gives them time for another job and maybe a second career when children have left home. They can be out and about. But it is the same technology, in the form of computers, which has forced retirement on their husbands who are then ready to 'come home' as their wives move out into the market place. The result is often two people going in opposite directions at an even deeper level as well.

*The Rich–Poor Gap*

There seems to be no country in the world where the gap between the rich and poor is not increasing; while this is primarily due to selfishness, technology makes it easier. It need not be so, of course, and the time has come for moral people to think about it, to speak out and to do something about it.

*Advertising*

Advertisers are actively engaged in selling good products and bad ones. Constant survey results, fed into computers, are sharpening the battle for our minds and our money. The per capita consumption of advertising in United States is $200 per year, but it is money which returns to the company – people's money: otherwise companies would not be doing it. The media for this process are print, radio and TV – all gifts of modern technology. The process is worth thinking about.

*Use of Time*

Time could end up being for the 90s what money was for the 80s; it is about to be felt as the scarcest commodity we have. While we all feel the gradual disappearance of the luxuries of time, like relaxed conversation or strolling in the park, let us be aware that even the essentials of time, such as family mealtime, mourning time and even time to listen to one another, could soon be out of reach.

Time could be for the 90s what money was for the 80s.

Technology promises us more time, but in fact we seem to have less of it. One magazine recently tells how some parents put a card under a child's pillow, which read, 'I wish I were here to tuck you in.' The explosion of information means that most of us have more of it than we can handle usefully and with peace of mind. The speeded-up schedule of modern life can lead to hyper-tension, ulcers, heart disease or dependence on drugs.

Many thinking people have climbed down, or stayed put on the promotional ladder for the good of their families and for their own good; some things are not worth the price.

*A New Language*

There is no sign that the march of technology can be stopped or reversed – even if we wanted to stop it. One cannot disinvent TV nor force the world to stop buying videos; nor should one. Technology constantly offers more control – or the illusion of it – just a button away. Even if not always spoken aloud, its language is something like this:

More is better than less;
now is better than later;
sound is better than silence;
more control is better than less;
'for now' is better than 'forever';
doing is better than being;
care of self is better than concern for others;
faster is better than slower
and new is better than older.

No wonder it moves forward so quickly!

## Reviewing Chapter Two

Was there anything in this chapter to which you could immediately relate from your own experience?
Were there any new ideas which you found puzzling or worrisome?
Did you find in this chapter anything of benefit to you in your particular role as a Christian?
*You may find it helpful to make a note of any thoughts from this chapter which you would like to remember.*

## Questions for discussion in your group

1. In areas like ecology, family, electronic media, travel, education, marriage, poor-rich divide, advertising, etc., the technological age seems to bring:
i. benefits
ii. harmful effects.
Have a look at some of the above areas and consider the benefits and harmful effects. Tell stories, share memories and give personal reflections.
2. Can the benfits of living in a technological society be maximised and the harmful effects minimised?

# Chapter 3:
# How technology affects religion and faith

Faith, like love, is in our hearts. Like love again, it will manifest itself visibly; it will show itself and be seen. Good manners, kind deeds, gentle words, and gift-giving are usually signs of love.

Faith usually shows itself visibly in altars, candles, ritual, personal and organised action for others; this is *religion* – faith on the outside.

Faith itself is basically a deep, trustful obedience to God's Word, based on one's experience of being personally loved by God.

*Secularisation*

Technology touches both religion and faith, more or less, in four ways:

1. In a highly technological society, governments and civil authorities gradually take over institutions, like hospitals and schools, which were previously under the control of churches. These religiously high-profile places, external presences of the Church, then cease to be signs of faith, even if they still hold the original saint's name for a long time.

God seems to be withdrawing. The influence of God appears to be slipping away.

These external signs of the Church's presence gave it more influence in society, and the Church was free to choose the type of people who controlled and served each institution. But, much more importantly, these buildings and their work were usually a reminder of the Church's faith and a visible support for those who had faith themselves. Their movement out of Church control is inevitably one less obvious sign and reminder of God's presence in the world. We call this *Institutional Secularisation.*

2. For people of faith, their religion helps them to make sense of life, to put life together; it gives them some

overarching meaning, helping them to hold all life's bits in one meaningful whole. Faith gives many people the assurance that the world is in God's safe hands, that the cosmos is sacred, and that he or she has a place in this overall God-ordered universe. It may be oversimplifying it to say that, for many, God is even like a great clockmaker, clockminder and clockwinder, above and outside of the world.

Technology makes this position less easy to maintain, as science continues to explain previously unexplained facts. It becomes increasingly difficult to say, 'God does it.' There appears to be less and less need now to posit God to explain the work of nature, as science pushes the frontiers of human knowledge back further with each new discovery. As we gain more and more control of the universe and of nature, the area of the sacred appears to be decreasing and that of the secular increasing; God seems to be withdrawing.

It becomes increasingly difficult to say, 'God does it.'

This is not atheism, which is a deliberate 'rational' decision that God does not exist. Rather it is very often an experience in good people's lives that, despite their best efforts, the God they knew, or the influence of God which they thought they experienced, appears to be slipping away.

We all recall our grandparents telling us stories about elves, mermaids, fairies and ghosts. Many large groups of people still believe in similar myths. The world of technology kills myths like these very easily. Similar large groups have made their lives meaningful with great overarching ideas, like communism, socialism, democracy and others, but again the technological revolution – especially the communications media – has forced people to question their every idea and the ideologies which sustained them. Referring to changes in China, and using religious language, a journalist wrote, 'The reforms are secularising the party and gutting its core belief structure.' (*Far East Economic Review*, 27.10.88)

As a result of this – what we call *Cognitive Secularisation* – people are forced to find more private, personal meaning to hold their lives together, and to find faith within themselves. There was a time when Church leaders were expected to say something final about most things, and they often tried to give overall umbrella-answers to people's search for meaning. They cannot do it now, since every science has its own answers with fewer points of reference to other disciplines. Like other spheres of human life, religion too can become autonomous and lose its point of connectedness with the world.

3. For many of us, faith and the Church offer guidance about how we act; the Church for many is still a teacher of law. But science and technology have taken over all or part of this role in the lives of many sincere people; science gives answers to many questions once answered by religion, and so, guidance is being sought there too. People's values and guiding principles for behaviour are becoming less religious, or at least the religious guidance comes more from individual consciences alone, not from religious institutions. One danger is that society loses all moral direction while personal ambitions and desires become its sole motivation.

This is called *Normative* or *Ethical Secularisation.*

4. Finally, the scientific revolution could have the effect of lessening people's personal experience of God. It is difficult to know if this is happening, and there is no clear evidence that it is. Perhaps men and women are still meeting God in the fast world of technology too. We have not enough evidence on this very private matter to be sure one way or another, but perhaps, as Bertrand Russell said, 'Fishermen in sailing boats believe more easily in God than fishermen in motor boats.' If it is true that fewer people meet God in their hearts today, then *Experiential Secularisation* is taking place.

However we name it, there seems to be a growing distance between religion and the world shaped by science and technology, or at least between church-linked religion and people's experience of life today. Religion seems to be withdrawing from the everyday world into a Sunday-world or into a very private concern. The integrating and world-shaping influence, which religion should have on people and society, seems to be decreasing as technology's presence increases. Yet, at the same time, small groups are trying to re-unite faith and life through active concern for justice, human development and peace today.

*Secularism*

The challenge to purify our faith, which the world of technology gives us, is not an easy one. We may have to let go of earlier images of God. Instead of doing this, many Christians live with a shallow or absent faith, but still keep up the outward signs like church-going and other rituals. Their daily lives are lived as if God did not exist, even if they still practise some religious behaviour once a week or even more often. In a way it is practical atheism without claiming or naming it.

> The main danger to religion is not unbelief but shallow belief.

Michael Paul Gallagher put it this way: 'The main danger to religion is not unbelief but shallow belief – a religion without challenge and without depth, on the margin of life.'

Another danger today is that conflicting values – religious and secular – be held by the same person. This is a sort of split-levelled life, one of 'faith' and the other of real life. In this case it is not real faith, since it is isolated from one's day-to-day existence.

The word *secularism* is often used to describe this. Jesus spoke of it: 'It is not those who say to me Lord, Lord, who will enter the Kingdom of Heaven, but those who do the will of my Father.' (Mt 7:21)

*Fundamentalism*

The technological revolution questions our faith and challenges us to purify and deepen it. This is not easy because there is a lot of change, uncertainty, or at least ambiguity, which confuses. Everything seems to be moving and questions pile upon us. Many people take a conscious or unconscious decision to close their minds to the confusion, and settle for a simplistic faith and a naïve belief in the immediacy of God. They are tired of struggle and they reach for a stability that makes them feel comfortable. They seek certainty in everything and they almost identify God with a devotion, an apparition, the Bible, a medal, a saint, a Church leader or one doctrine. This is called *fundamentalism.*

> They seem to say that without religion there are no answers, and that with religion there are no questions.

It must be distinguished from the position of a person with a solid and simple faith, which is usually far from rigid and which enables that person to hold deep religious certainties, while living with less than total clarity in the details of belief and practice.

You may have noticed the apparent success of fundamentalist TV preachers in generating 'religious' experiences. If, however, you listen carefully, you will notice that they are not challenging their audiences with the death-resurrection mystery of Christ; they are selling consumerist success in selective biblical images. They are using both the Bible and technology to satisfy people's search for certainty and for material prosperity in the modern world. Fundamentalists thrive on the control-and-consume message which technology favours and which may transform religious realities into new consumer goods.

Fundamentalists believe more and more in less and less, while secularism believes less and less in more and more. In a way, they are saying that without religion there are no answers, and that with religion there are no questions.

*Unbelief*

One must not too readily accuse oneself of loss of faith, or unbelief, just because the age of technology may call for a new kind of faith, a deeper one. A feeling of unbelief is often just an honest acceptance that one cannot believe in the way one believed before. Or it may be just facing the fact that one cannot bubble with faith as some others – especially Fundamentalists – seem to do. Or it may also be the lack of awareness that faith is as varied as people. Your faith is uniquely yours, and yours at this time. Because it is not what it was some years ago, or not like that of your friends, is no reason to accuse yourself of atheism.

Faith is never a comfortable certainty; to have faith is to have doubts. Only the Secularists and the Fundamentalists have no doubts. To have faith is to have doubts but to live and act with confidence just the same. God's hiddenness is part of Christian faith, and even to feel the pain of God's apparent absence, is an act of faith in itself. We all have occasional vivid religious experiences when we 'meet' God, but this is not every day. A religion that does not affirm God's hiddenness is not true: 'Truly, you are a hidden God.' (Is 45:15) The prophet is clear about this and, in fact, the original Hebrew for 'hidden' is 'self-concealing.'

To have faith is to have doubts but to live and act with confidence just the same.

God is to be found and known in symbols, but God is not identical with them. The world of technology does not limit God's ability to symbolise the Divine presence to us, as we will see later. But these symbols reveal God as incomprehensible *mystery*, 'mystery' in the sense of something which is so deep that it is endlessly rich. We must learn to accept therefore that every symbol or sacrament of God's presence is also a symbol or sacrament of God's absence, and every encounter with God's Word is also an encounter with silence. St Paul reminds us of this: 'Now we are seeing a dim reflection in a mirror; but then we shall be seeing face to face.' (1 Cor 13:12) We meet God in the very act of trying to resolve the many ambiguities of modern life, even when we fail to resolve them.

Our knowledge of God is never a possession; it is always a search in 'living hope' (1 Pet 1:3) and a willingness to be taken hold of by God (cf Phil 3:12). Perhaps technology teaches us these deeper truths in a new way and is therefore a blessing, in that it makes us find God more deeply than we had before. A long time ago, St Augustine said that when we say we know God, it is not God we know. Before the true God, we need a deep respect for God's utter incomprehensibility and a healthy hesitance in approaching the Divine. It is only on our knees, metaphorically, that we can meet God, and in our willingness to be loved by, and to love God, that we will come to know God.

### *Does Faith Change?*

Most adult Catholics can recall when the object of our faith was regarded as a collection of 'revealed truths,' written in the Bible and taught in the Church. If this were faith, then it could never change. However, faith is much more beautiful than this and because it is multifaceted, it is impossible to express all its aspects in one phrase. It is basically the way in which we accept God's love, and the quality of that acceptance. This can and does change, and is different in each person, even in the same person at different times. When technology revolutionises human experience, we must expect that faith might undergo a revolution too – perhaps a needed one. 'Science can purify religion from error and superstition; religion can purify science from idolatry and false absolutes. Each can draw the other into a wider world, a world in which both can flourish ... The uses of science have, on more than one occasion, proven massively destructive, and the reflections on religion have too often been sterile. We need each other to be what we need to be, what we are called to be.'

–*John Paul II* to the Director of the Vatican Observatory
cf. *Osservatore Romano* 26.10.89

## Reviewing Chapter Three

Was there anything in this chapter to which you could immediately relate from your own experience?
Were there any new ideas which you found puzzling or worrisome?
Did you find in this chapter anything of benefit to you in your particular role as a Christian?
*You may find it helpful to make a note of any thoughts from this chapter which you would like to remember.*

## Questions for discussion in your group

1. What pressures do you feel living out your own faith in a technological society?
2. Does the technological society make it harder to have faith?
3. From your own experience, do you agree that to have faith is to have doubts?

*Part Two*
# Being Human Now

# Chapter 4: Technology changes people

### *Introduction*

In all areas of life, the 'cruising speed' of humankind has been more or less constant for six thousand years. The Napoleonic armies moved at exactly the same speed as those of the pharoahs – the speed of their horses. In the nineteenth century, this speed was increased fourfold by the steam engine. But today, with supersonic flights and manned rockets, a radical change has taken place. Technology has modified the concept of movement and our experience of it.

### *Technology Changes People*

Nearly every year, electronics come up with something new, which very soon touches and changes our environment. Soon the changes go deeper – into ourselves; we too are changed. There were a few hundred computers in the world in 1968, and 80,000 ten years later, mostly in the hands of specialists or big companies. Now our children play with them and graduate in computer technology; their attitudes are being changed just as their parents' attitude must change too, especially when the same computer displaces them at work.

Let us recall here some of the language, the message of technology: more is better than less; now is preferable to later; faster better than slower; instancy rather than delay, and control must be chosen above acceptance. It also seems to say that movement is preferable to stability, action to reflection and care for oneself to concern for others. The advertisements say all this and also that 'yes' is better than 'no.' It appears that this language is permeating our attitudes and that the human person is changing significantly because of it.

### *Two Languages*

As dedicated scientists work patiently in the laboratory, they naturally work from principles which help them transfer information into useful technology. The information behind the telescope, for example, has now been applied to enable non-intrusive 'key-hole' surgery. The unspoken language of successful technological advances might be expressed like this:

things can always be improved;
questions are always productive;
analysis is always useful;
experiment is always desirable;
all problems have a solution;
innovation is better than repetition.

The successful scientist has to be convinced that mastery is better than mere participation, and that control always improves on contemplation. All of this is productive thinking; it works – for technology.

Imagine applying this thinking to human growth and think if it would produce happy friendships, lasting marriages and balanced societies. We often have to live with situations which cannot be improved, with questions which cannot be vocalised, and with relationships which are better not analysed. There are sane limits to experiment in human situations, and innovative approaches could be disastrously irreversible. The principles and language of technology are good for the trade of technology, but could be very harmful when applied without reflection to the human family. Yet it appears that this is happening, and that it is resulting in new attitudes which, in turn, produce a new type of person. And not only is this person emerging, but he or she is moving from an experience of identity and belonging to one of personal insecurity and isolation.

### *The Individual Has Emerged*

When people travelled less, read less about other places and other ways of life, when they saw less than they do now through video and TV, a strong feeling of belonging existed. It is of course a long time ago since people lived fully in geographical, psychological and ideological 'villages.' In fact it may be that the big changes began when the first troubadour left his own village and arrived in another. Barriers were gradually broken down and belonging ceased to be as strong as before. Modern technology has speeded up this process to an uncomfortable level for most of us. As the theologian, David Tracy, says: 'A fact seldom admitted by the moderns ... is that there is no longer *a* centre with margins. There are *many* centres. Pluralism is an honourable but sometimes too easy way of admitting this fact.' (*Concilium*, 1990/1)

Together with the emergence of the individual, what McLuhan calls 're-tribalisation' is taking place as small and large single-issue groups band together in self-interest and self-defence, e.g. women, ethnic groups, etc.

On the positive side, videos offer new educational opportunities and unimagined perspectives to some people whose windows on the world have long been shuttered by government control. Another benefit is that the individual, well known and maybe well-labelled in his own home place, once had limited space in which to deviate from social and cultural expectations. The reward was security but the price for non-conformism or for creative people was high. The troubadour was prepared to pay the price and so were the many social activists of history. Technology favours creativity, non-conformism, less belonging and makes us all troubadours most of the time.

Depending on how you look at it, the individual is now more free or more isolated, more independent or less supported, more mobile or less secure. Whatever way you see it, it is clear that technology has contributed to making the individual more than just a member of a group. This has positive and problematic consequences for his or her personhood and experience of God.

Let us now look at some of the characteristics of people in the age of technology and then see what the Christian message has to say to their situation.

## Reviewing Chapter Four

Was there anything in this chapter to which you could immediately relate from your own experience?
Were there any new ideas which you found puzzling or worrisome?
Did you find in this chapter anything of benefit to you in your particular role as a Christian?
*You may find it helpful to make a note of any thoughts from this chapter which you would like to remember.*

## Questions for discussion in your group

1. Look again at the language of technology on page 32. Do you agree that this language is permeating our thinking and our attitudes in an irreversible way?
2. It is suggested that the technological society gives us freedom at the cost of loneliness/isolation. Is this your experience?

# Chapter 5: To be human and Christian today

*Anxious Self-awareness*

Our parents and grandparents usually had a healthy enough awareness of themselves; they often manifested significant aggression when their rights were infringed. But mostly they also knew their 'place.' They were able to accept this too, however limited a place it may have been, because society said they must. The socially enforced acceptance of one's place, role and situation contributed to a limited self-awareness, which had its benefits but also its problems.

Things are different for most of us now, since geographical, psychological, intellectual, social and cultural mobility are favoured by the modern world. People travel in their minds by thinking independent thoughts, thanks to modern education; they read what they like, visit other countries and question cultural 'givens' easily. All this both contributes to and flows from a heightened self-awareness.

People feel they are threatened by the isolation and alienation they experience.

Courses in awareness, personal enrichment programmes, and floods of magazines help towards a high level of self-consciousness. And this is so true that no 'village,' organisation, group, nation or church can entirely corset the modern person now. Spontaneous and individual creativity is a popular virtue and people want their uniqueness accepted and acknowledged today.

This is also true of groups. Women in general are no longer willing to take second-class treatment in society or in the church. Minority groups are loud in pointing to their identity and towards any signs of discrimination, while the human rights movement has taken off forcefully.

The result seems to be a high level of anxiety, due to the lack of personal support. People feel they are threatened by the isolation and alienation they experience.

And this anxiety has some serious psychosomatic effects which keep doctors and psychiatrists busier than before. Let us now see what the Gospel has to say about self-awareness.

### *The Challenge of the Christian Message*

A healthy level of self-awareness is vital for mature living at any time, but more than ever today. This is especially true of one's Christian identity. Here is how St Paul expresses his: 'The life that I am now living, subject to the limitation of human nature, I am living in faith, faith in the Son of God who loved me and gave himself for me.' (Gal 2:20)

This fact of being personally loved by God is the deepest source of an anxiety-free self awareness for a person in any age. With it we can link these anxiety-reducing words of St Peter: 'Unload all your worries on him, since he is looking after you.' (1 Pet 4:7)

It is pointless to pray for freedom from all anxiety, since a healthy level of anxiety is part of survival and growth, but there is a basic peace which the world of technology cannot take from us, if we claim it: 'Peace is my bequest to you; my own peace I give you, a peace which the world cannot give, this is my gift to you. Do not let your heart be troubled nor afraid.' (Jn 14:27)

Much anxiety today comes from the competitiveness of modern life, as each one seeks his or her own advantage. St Paul summarises the teaching of Jesus by describing his own life: 'I try to be helpful to everyone at all times, not anxious for my own advantage.' (1 Cor 10:33)

There is no better formula for freedom from hurtful anxiety, than active concern to help others; too much self-awareness and self concern is a formula for unhappiness. To put oneself into active service for minority and under-privileged groups by joining appropriate organisations is not only living as a Christian ought to, but it is choosing a very healthy stance for survival and victory over the tensions of modern life. St Peter puts it this way:
'Above all preserve an intense love for each other, since

love covers over many a sin. Welcome each other into your houses without grumbling. Each one of you has received a special grace, so like good stewards responsible for all these varied graces of God, put it at the service of others.' (1 Pet 7:10)

*With Rising Expectations*

Science and technology tell us that things can always be moved forward. They more or less say that ways of doing things can be improved by research, invention and innovation. In most cases this is true, even if 'improved' does not always mean better for people. The next dishwasher and the next nuclear submarine will be improvements on the present ones. Next year's car and next year's aircraft carriers will be more sophisticated than previous ones. All of these are improvements but are they humanly beneficial?

Technology favours now rather than later.

Based on the belief that the Gross National Product can and must always grow, governments are on constant trial to make each year's bigger than the last one. The word 'growth' has taken on sacred connotations without any moral tone. For many years the word 'future' generated the same hopes for better things, but now many people – especially the young – are beginning to link the future with less than good news.

However, the language behind this – 'more is always there' – has gradually and for the foreseeable future, permeated the modern psyche. People see the world as a sort of supermarket where one has only to shop around to get something better.

Technology is essentially functional, it is directed towards making what is immediately useful. It puts much more emphasis on expectations than on awareness, on what is easily visible than on what is less foreseeable and on instinct than on rational response. It favours now rather than later. For this reason there is a constant danger that the modern person will drink or drug him or herself out of awareness, or spend the time shopping – which is the same thing.

Has the Christian message something to say about constantly rising expectations? Let us look at this.

*The Challenge of the Christian Message*

God made the world for our use, benefit and enjoyment and 'he saw that it was good.' (Gen 1:25) But it was made for our *shared* enjoyment. It would never be lawful to have unlimited expectations for one's own benefit. Jesus told a story about a man who did not steal, but worked hard and was blessed with more wealth than he needed: 'There was once a rich man who, having had a good harvest from his land, thought to himself, "What am I to do? I have not enough room to store my crops." Then he said, "This is what I will do: I will pull down my barns and build bigger ones, and store all my grain and my goods in them, and I will say to my soul: My soul, you have plenty of good things laid by for many years to come; take things easy, eat, drink, have a good time." But God said to him, "Fool! This very night the demand will be made for your soul; and this hoard of yours, whose will it be then?" So it is when a man stores up treasure for himself in place of making himself rich in the sight of God.' (Lk 12:13-21)

His unlimited expectations had made him 'store up' and 'for himself.' It was for this that God called him a fool. We know that neither Jesus nor St Paul calls us to poverty but only to limit our expectations to what we need and what is available: 'We brought nothing into the world, and we can take nothing out of it; but as long as we have food and clothing, let us be content with that. People who long to be rich are a prey to temptation; they get trapped into all sorts of foolish and dangerous ambitions which eventually plunge them into ruin and destruction. The love of money is the root of all evils and there are some who, pursuing it, have wandered away from the faith, and so given their souls any number of fatal wounds.' (1 Tim 6:7-11)

The exercise of unlimited expectations for oneself can be especially immoral in a time when millions lack basic necessities. Each time I purchase what I do not really need, I further the consumer society which in turn constantly favours the wealthier 20% of the world. At very least, if I have money that I genuinely do not need, it belongs to those who have so many of their fundamental needs unmet. 'If anyone is well off in worldly possessions and sees his brother in need but closes his heart to him, how can the love of God be remaining in him? Children, our love must be not words or mere talk, but something active and genuine. This will be the proof that we belong to the truth.' (1 Jn 3:17,18)

What I don't need isn't mine – no matter what my expectations and no matter how I earn it.

*Controlling and Consuming*

Technology has taught us that things can be captured and controlled. Electricity was first discovered and then very usefully controlled and now nuclear energy can fuel our powerplants or be exploded with great precision. While we have not yet controlled the weather, we can go far towards predicting it, and airconditioning has in some way a hold on how it touches us. Much of nature has been 'tamed' and technology says we can and must eventually control or tame everything.

Technology has taught us that things can be captured and controlled.

Much of the modern person's approach to life is one of 'control and consume.' It is true of distance as we travel, knowledge as we write theses, of food as we eat and of gadgets as we throw them away to get ones with easier, quicker and more effective control. So much of this has been beneficial for human living, but now, thinking people wonder if we might leave our children a desert which we created by consuming the world's natural resources. Can the cake be cut forever?

The attitudinal effects are perhaps the more serious ones as the grab-and-get approach of technology moves into the area of human relations. Science thinks of everything in terms of its use, rarely in terms of its beauty; and so a beautiful waterfall may have to be harnessed into a hydro-electric power station. Other people's beauty is similarly defined in terms of its 'use-to-me' and so those who are no use to others – the old, the handicapped – count for little or nothing in many modern societies.

It can easily happen that God too can be instrumentalised. Without saying it, with our technologically-trained attitudes, we may be asking 'what use is God to me?' Meditation has become more a means of lowering blood pressure than of reaching intimacy with God. Each succeeding course in 'spirituality' can become an unconscius attempt to capture God. Courses on how to become a contemplative sometimes forget that contemplation is God's gift and cannot be engineered outside of God's time.

War has often been an attempt to control other people. Has it now become an attempt to consume the arms which big companies have made?

Let us reflect on what the Christian message has to say about the danger of being consumed by consuming.

*The Challenge of the Christian Message*

The Christian attitude towards all things is not one of control and consume; it is one of use, enjoy and share:

'Instruct those who are rich in this world's goods that they should not be proud and should set their hopes not on money, which is untrustworthy, but on God who gives us richly all that we need for our happiness. They are to do good and be rich in good works, generous in giving and always ready to share – this is the way they can amass a good capital sum for the future if they want to possess the only life that is real.' (1 Tim 6:17-19)

When the advertisements tell us loudly and in colour that some new product, or all of them together, might be just what we need, the word of God warns us: 'Human beings do not live on bread alone but on every word that comes from the mouth of God.' (Deut 8:3)

Maybe we are being pushed at times to pursue our shallow needs to the neglect of deeper ones. 'Watch and be on your guard against avarice of any kind, for life does not consist in possessions, even when someone has more than he needs.' (Lk 12:15) In the Beatitudes, his policy speech, Jesus tells us: 'Blessed are the gentle; they shall have the earth as inheritance.' (Mt 5:4)

As we use technology to 'tame' nature and at times to consume it recklessly, even common sense is beginning to remind us that a more gentle approach might be better. The resources of the earth are not endless and there is already a danger that this, or the next generation might not leave any inheritance behind for later ones. The ecologists serve us well when they remind us of this.

Then St John gives us wisdom. It should be noted that he uses the word 'world' in the sense of a selfish use of things; he is not talking about all of God's beautiful creation. 'Do not love the world or what is in the world. If any one does love the world, the love of the father finds no place in him, because everything there is in the world – disordered bodily desires, disordered desires of the eyes, pride in possession – is not from the Father but is from the world. And the world, with all its disordered desires, is passing away. But whoever does the will of God remains for ever.' (1 Jn 2:15-17)

This is sound advice to a generation being told that desires and possessions are the meaning of life.

*Questioning Authority*

> Intelligent questioning of authority is a worthwhile thing to do.

History shows us that secular authority needs to be questioned. It has been frighteningly abused down through the centuries. Despots have controlled and killed whole populations because their authority was not accepted. And they claim the same authority over the armies which are still killing. Millions of young men and women have been drafted and killed in wars about which they knew little and in which they had no personal interest.

All authority is losing ground today because prime ministers, politicians and priests can be demystified on radio or television. Technology encourages all of us to question the experts and those who claim a right to give final and binding answers. Only the Fundamentalists surrender blindly.

Intelligent questioning of authority is a worthwhile thing to do; it is indeed an obligation based on the fact that God alone is God. But there is an end to questioning and we must ask, 'When does a question become a statement of personal arrogance or an attack on lawful authority?' Just because no one is a final expert in even one field of technology, does not mean that someone cannot give spiritual and moral guidance today.

*The Challenge of the Christian Message*

Basic to our living by faith is an acceptance of God's authority, God's will for our happiness, and God's word guiding us towards it. After our belief in the Divine love for us, there is the bottom line: 'Why do you call me, "Lord, Lord" and not do what I say?' 'Everyone who comes to me and listens to my words and acts on them – I will show you what such a person is like. Such a person is like the man who, when he built a house, dug, and dug deep, and laid the foundations on rock; when the river was in flood it bore down on that house but could not shake it, it was so well built. But someone who listens and does nothing is like the man who built a house on soil, with no foundations; as soon as the river bore down on it, it collapsed; and what a ruin that house became!' (Lk 6:46-49)

When Jesus founded his Church, he told its leaders, and its members as well: 'Anyone who listens to you listens to me; anyone who rejects you rejects me, and those who reject me, reject the one who sent me.' (Lk 10:16)

That this is not a blank cheque for an irresponsible use of ecclesiastical power is clear from St Peter's words to church leaders in his time: they are reminded that they must reflect and mediate the care of God for people: 'Be the shepherds of the flock of God that is entrusted to you: watch over it, not simply as a duty but gladly, because God wants it; not for sordid money, but because you are eager to do it. Never be a dictator over any group that is put in your charge, but be an example that the whole flock can follow. When the chief shepherd appears, you will be given the crown of unfading glory.' (1 Pet 5:3–4)

When authority is accepted as a service of others and listens deeply to those it serves, it can help people to find the will of God, which is always the best way to live lovingly and productively together. In the letter to the Ephesian community, we find the following advice about sharing our talents in truth and love together. 'If we live by the truth and in love, we shall grow in all ways into Christ, who is the head by whom the whole body is fitted and joined together, every joint adding its own strength, for each separate part to work according to its function. So the body grows until it has built itself up, in love.' (Eph 4:16–17) Leadership coordinates this sharing.

An active and intelligent loyalty to authentic leadership is both God's will and human wisdom.

*Hesitating About Common Purpose*

While history has had its great prophets who fruitfully questioned community decisions and directions, in general, most progress has been reached when people came together to achieve a common goal. Families have survived because they buried their individual needs and differences in order to work together. Neighbourhoods began controlling crime as they set up neighbourhood watch groups, even if they could not cooperate on other things. With the insight of their founders or foundresses, religious groups have come together around a common goal – a mission – and achieved great things for deprived and suffering people, at significant cost to themselves.

> It is difficult to get people to follow a common vision or goal together.

This is not so easy for the modern person because

technology tends to move easily from specialisation into strong individualism. It is only in the approaching post-modern era that leaders in various sciences are beginning to pull down the walls of specialisation and to link up with other sciences – even religion – for the benefit of all. The interdependence of economics and morality is an obvious example. In general however, the sense of common purpose is lacking today and so it is difficult to get people to follow a common vision or goal together. God's word has wisdom on this point.

*The Challenge of the Christian Message*

We are close to the centre of the Christian message when we say that God wants us to work together in building God's Church and the Kingdom of God. This means forgetting one's private agenda from time to time and using one's special gifts for the benefit of our common mission:
'In the light of the grace I have received I want to urge each one among you not to exaggerate his real importance. Each of you must judge himself soberly by the standard of the faith God has given him. Just as each of our bodies has several parts and each part has a separate function, so all of us, in union with Christ, form one body, and as parts of it we belong to each other. Our gifts differ according to the grace given us. If your gift is prophecy, then use it as your faith suggests; if administration, then use it for administration; if teaching, then use it for teaching. Let the preachers deliver sermons, the almsgivers give freely, the officials be diligent, and those who do works of mercy do them cheerfully.' (Rom 12:3-8)

Then, despite the difficulties of getting together with others when technology tends to disintegrate communal effort, Jesus reminds us that wherever sincere people come together in his name, he is present: 'Where two or three meet in my name, I am there among them.' (Mt 18:20)

People who bring people together in a sharing, and non-manipulative atmosphere, whether it is to play tennis or to pray, to share a meal or to help the homeless, to reconcile or to recreate, are probably the most important people today when estrangement is the illness of our age.

St Paul appealed to the Roman colony at Philippi for the unity of corporate humility, based on the model of Jesus: 'I appeal to you, make my joy complete by being of a single mind, one in love, one in heart and one in mind. Nothing is to be done out of jealousy or vanity; instead, out of humility of mind everyone should give preference to others, everyone pursuing not selfish interests but those of others. Make your own the mind of Christ Jesus.' (Phil 2:3-5)

The very survival of humanity may depend on the willingness of people to do this today.

*Fragmented and Competitive*

Technology functions best with units, single bits, bytes and with their interaction on one another. It is dealing with analysis and division, rather than synthesis and wholeness, because best results come from this approach. It will readily pull things apart and rearrange the bits if they function better that way. This has an effect on people too, who find themselves reduced to bits that can have different functions at different times. 'Nothing could be further from the spirit of the new technology than "a place for everything and everything in its place."' (Marshall McLuhan)

It is stressful to live in an impersonal world.

Social life was once an integrating experience; people knew people around them. But now, a person has as many social selves as groups in whose opinion he or she is interested. The person sitting beside you on the way to work can be an active pedophile, a born-again Christian, an escaped criminal or a nun in slacks. This means less support for one's identity, with a higher likelihood of competition and conflict, as one feels one has to guard a purse, defend a job or resist the pressure to join a new sect.

It is stressful to live in an impersonal world but also in a world which seems to favour action over reflection. Relaxed reflection is the best answer to the stress which comes from modern life, but this seems to be the very thing which is hard to practice today. Technology is action-oriented with beneficial and problematic results; the latter would be less prominent if time for reflection were easier to find.

Let us look at the Christian answer to modern fragmentation.

*The Challenge of the Christian Message*

Nothing gives a feeling of belonging and of identity like the experience of being very personally loved. People who have felt this, have endured almost unbelievable suffering and even undergone death with a deep peace. This was the case with Jesus and he assures us that the same gift and experience is offered to each of us: 'As the father has loved me, so I have loved you.' (Jn 15:9)

St Paul, who suffered so much – imprisoned, flogged, stoned, shipwrecked and deserted by friends – tells us what sustained him through it all: 'I have been crucified with Christ living in me. The life I am now living subject to the limitations of human nature, I am living in faith, faith in the Son of God who loved me and gave himself for me.' (Gal 2:20-21)

In prayer we too can all gradually find this sense of integration, wholeness and identity.

It is then a matter of letting this same love of God flow through us to others in practical action for their happiness. If we remain in a pseudo-contemplation of God's love for us, without passing it on to others, we are like a person trying to continually breathe in without breathing out. This is disintegrative and self-destructive. 'This is my commandment: love one another, as I have loved you. No one can have greater love than to lay down his life for his friends. You are my friends if you do what I command you.' (Jn 15:12-13) This is the simple secret of an integrated life.

And Jesus gave us a vivid way to measure just how integrated our lives really are called to be: 'So then, if you are bringing your offering to the altar and there remember that your brother has something against you, leave your offering there before the altar, go be reconciled with your brother first, and then come back and present your offering.' (Mt 5:23-24)

The modern person too can escape from a feeling of fragmentation, competition, conflict and confused identity, only by accepting this.

*Fearful of Commitment*

One's own enjoyment, 'development' or 'fulfilment' in the sense of self-enhancement, can easily become an end in life, as people accept the promise of technology that happiness is just over the next hill or at the next beauty salon. It is not a long step from this to think that marital happiness is always with the next partner or that the present partner should be shed, because he or she conflicts with one's career.

Commitment then centres around expectations, desires and rewards, rather than having its origin in generous loving choice, based on reasonable compatibility. And so, relationships and marriages last just as long as they reward individual expectations; fidelity has no real meaning. After all, no scientist stays faithful to an experiment or a piece of technology which does not reward him or her by results that are measurable. A fruitful technological approach is to keep one's options open – a perfect formula for living unhappily and marrying ever after, if it is applied to relationships.

Many commitments are likely to be tentative, that is 'until something better turns up.'

It seems that today many commitments – to jobs or to people – are likely to be tentative, that is, until 'something better' turns up. This approach can sometimes work for jobs and that is why loyalty to organisations has a short life today; it is nearly always conditional. But applied to relationships, the approach has built-in frustration, and people discover only too late that the punishment for selfish desire is to be enslaved by desire itself.

Let us now look at the Christian understanding of friendship and freedom and commitment.

*The Challenge of the Christian Message*

The central message of the Bible is God's faithful love for all people even when they disbelieved, rejected or scorned it. God had made a covenant – a promise to stay with them lovingly and mercifully no matter what; God did this and will always, as Jesus promised in a dramatic covenant: 'This cup is the new covenant in my blood which will be poured out for you.' (Lk 22:20) This is God's priceless, permanent and powerful promise of loving and unconditional fidelity to each of us.

The Christian life is our free response to the fidelity of God, for which God gives us the motive and the energy: 'You will have in you the strength based on his own glorious power, never to give in, but to bear anything joyfully.' (Col 1:11) and 'Do not give up if trials come; and keep on praying.' (Rom 12:12)

The real test of this fidelity to God is fidelity to one another, especially to those to whom we have publicly vowed it: 'This is why a man leaves his father and mother and becomes attached to his wife, and they become one flesh. They are no longer two, but one flesh. So then, what God has united human beings must not divide.' (Mt 19:5-6)

Of course, there are occasional situations where the commitment was not made freely in the first place. It may then be submitted to the church for assessment. In the case where one spouse walks away unfaithfully, there is a deep and demanding challenge to the innocent spouse to be faithful still: 'Everyone who divorces his wife and marries another is guilty of adultery, and the man who marries a woman divorced by her husband commits adultery.' (Lk 16:17) The disciples recognised that this was very demanding, and they said to him, 'If that is how things are between husband and wife, it is not advisable to marry.' But he replied, 'It is not everyone who can accept what I have said, but only those to whom it is granted.' (Mt 9:10-11) Of course this is a call to heroism – an ideal not everyone can reach.

The adult use of freedom is heroic because freedom is not the capacity for an endless revision of choice, but rather the ability to make deep choices and follow them.

*Moving From Fate to Choice*

Older cultures did not generate a high level of self-awareness apart from the group, as common purpose and mediating authorities were generally accepted. Most pre-modern persons did not feel, or a least did not activate, a desire to investigate, compete, control and consume and so they were less anxious and felt less threatened than people today. In the past, there was also less education, in the sense of learning to question. For a combination of these reasons, fate was more favoured than choice; what was given was preferred more often than what could be chosen. The accepted-past deeply influenced the present, and the future was often enough left to fate and to faith.

The technological revolution and its effects on the very core of human experience demand that the modern person moves not just from fate to a faith which served our parents well, but to a new kind of faith, a new experience of God.

In 1970, Walbert Buhlmann wrote, 'All the indications suggest that our times, so heavy with threats, will give rise to a purer religion ... we are watching the phenomenon of secularisation with anxiety. But anxiety is unprofitable and cannot alter reality ... We must change our defensive, fearful attitude into human and Christian love, and our polemics into dialogue. Secularisation could become an open door to evangelisation in today's world.' (*On the Situation of Faith*, p. 305)

## Reviewing Chapter Five

Was there anything in this chapter to which you could immediately relate from your own experience?
Were there any new ideas which you found puzzling or worrisome?
Did you find in this chapter anything of benefit to you in your particular role as a Christian?
*You may find it helpful to make a note of any thoughts from this chapter which you would like to remember.*

## Questions for discussion in your group

1. People are conscious of and concerned about their individuality in today's technological society. What is the outcome of this?
2. How can we be content in an age of unlimited expectation?
3. How can our deeper needs be met in an age when we are being pushed and persuaded to pursue our shallow needs?
4. On reflection, do you think we have a tendency towards making tentative commitments?
5. What, in your opinion, is the secret of an integrated life in our competitive technological society?

# *Part Three*
# Meeting God Now

Chapter 6:
God's new invitation

Chapter 7:
Responding to the invitation

Chapter 8:
Salvation now

# Chapter 6: God's new invitation

Many among us today feel less secure in our faith than we did some years ago; we were at least secure enough in our experience of God, that we did not feel the need to think about or to analyse it. God was just there and questions were not. For many thinking people now, this question *is* there, even if they do not want it and maybe even if they do not listen to it. Many of these people still keep up their religious practice in church or continue to pray very sincerely; others have dropped one or the other to some degree. And all this is far from atheism or a deliberate rejection of God. Some of us can say that, in our hearts, in our family life, among our friends and at our workplace, 'all day long I am taunted, "Where is your God?"'(Ps 137:4)

> There seems to be less need for a God.

Church leaders continue to exhort us, as they must, to believe, to pray and to sing our familiar and our new hymns. And of course we have always had our brief moments of doubt, but for some of us it is different now, and again we can say with the Psalmist: 'How could we sing a song of Yahweh on alien soil?' (Ps 137:4)

We grew up in a world where we knew there were unbelievers but basically our own world was a religiously familiar one; now it seems to be religiously 'alien' and we are amazed – even if we are happy – that some people can sing their religious songs with more enthusiasm than ever.

The technological revolution seems to have pushed God further away from us; science continues to improve human knowledge and to give more non-religious answers; there seems to be less need for a God who fills gaps in our knowledge, as psychiatrists do what priests once did, and professional counselling takes over from the confessional. Church leaders are more careful about giving ready-answers or any answers at all and when they do – in the limited area of their competence – fewer people are listening. All of this has little to do with being anti-religious and less to do with real atheism, but just the same it can be disturbing for believers.

*God's New Invitation*

Humankind is taking more and more command over the world, through the advances of technology. Although the advances of recent years are unprecedented, they are built on human discovery and human creativity which have been going on since the beginning. It is all a fulfilment of God's command to our first parents: 'God blessed them, saying to them, "Be fruitful, multiply, fill the earth and subdue it."' (Gen 1:28) Technology is being used to 'subdue' the earth and will continue to do so in ways we cannot foresee.

We are called to find God in a new way – everywhere and deeply.

St Paul, without knowing it, could also have foretold what was going to happen, as God calls humankind to a fuller, more responsible and more mature control of the world: 'As long as we were still under age, we were enslaved to the elemental principles of this world ... Formerly when you did not know God, you were kept in slavery to things which were not really gods at all.' (Gal 4:3,8)

While he was not referring to modern technology, it applies here too, since we may have seen God in a naïve way in things 'which were not really gods at all' and science has fortunately discouraged us from doing so. It is now clearer than ever that we have received the earth for our responsible use and that we are no longer enslaved to its 'elemental principles.' We are called to find God in a new way – no longer here and there, when we cannot answer a question about nature, but everywhere and deeply.

Deaf people see dancing and then they 'hear' the

music; maybe the modern person is called to see God's action in modern technology and then to hear the music of God's presence within it. Again, the technological revolution is neither an invitation nor a pointer to atheism, but rather a call to meet God more closely through a purified faith.

*Meeting and Knowing*

We can meet one another in basically two ways – functionally or lovingly, and of course, we can mix them. Mostly, in the office, at work, travelling, etc., we meet people functionally, when it helps one or both of us to communicate or to co-operate; this meeting has as its primary purpose something gained, something done or something exchanged. It is a healthy enough form of interchange, unless we meet others only to use them. On the other hand, we can meet people lovingly, that is in order to give something of ourselves to others for their benefit; it is an occasion to express concern or caring and perhaps to receive these in return.

> Encountering God as God is a willingness to be taken hold of by God.

There are also two ways of knowing: knowing things and people functionally or knowing them in and for themselves. Knowing in the first instance is always the way we know things like knives, forks, food, etc. Of necessity it is functional; it is for ourselves. Knowing in the second instance – always the way when we really care about another – takes much longer because it is deeper. We can know things and people functionally against their will by studying, weighing and measuring them, but to know someone more deeply, we depend on him or her; only by their free consent can we know them in this way, as their real selves are inside their external appearance. Perhaps it is best to call this *Encountering* instead of just meeting or knowing, i.e. both persons walk part of the way towards each other.

We have to care about, and approach persons lovingly, before we can know them in this deep way of encounter. Unless you sense that I care about you, you will not open to me; you will not allow me to really know you. If you think that I care about you, that is, love you, you will give me the privilege of meeting, encountering and knowing you at this very personal level. Unless and until you do this, no effort by me will enable me to really know you as you are; in this you are totally in control, totally in charge.

So, persons can meet persons-as-persons only with an attitude of reverence for and caring about the other. This is the beginning of friendship, which is far from a merely functional or forced meeting between two people.

It is in this way, and in this way only, that we can hope to meet God. As you can see, it is entirely different from the language of technology.

*Preparing for Encounter*

God is not an object; God is a person; three persons in fact. For this reason, any approach to God in order to merely know, comprehend, control or use God must fail, even as it will fail when approaching another human being in this way. We have all experienced the beautiful and endless depths within another person whom we have lovingly and patiently encountered; how much more so with God: 'How rich and deep are the wisdom and the knowledge of God! We cannot reach to the root of his decisions or his ways. Who has ever known the mind of the Lord? Who has ever been his adviser? Who has given anything to him, so that his presents come only as a debt returned? Everything there is comes from him and is caused by him and exists for him. To him be glory for ever! Amen.' (Rom 11:33-36)

No matter how close one gets to God, God cannot be experienced directly or completely.

No matter how close one gets to God, God cannot be experienced directly or completely. We can only experience God's *nearness*, or what the Bible calls God's *glory*. While we experience the light and penetrating warmth of the sun, it always remains out there and beyond us. Similarly, God's experienced presence, or immanence, does not take away from his transcendence in any way. God always remains beyond our control and beyond our words, even when we have deep spiritual experiences of the divine.

Let us say this prayer with St Augustine as he searched for God; say it deeply and perhaps repeat it:

> You have made us for yourself
> and our hearts are restless till they rest in you.
> Grant me, O Lord, to know
> which is the soul's first movement toward you –
> to implore your aid or to utter its praise of you;
> and whether it must know you
> before it can implore.
> For it would seem clear
> that no one can call upon you
> without knowing you,
> for if he did, he might invoke another than you,
> knowing you not.
> Yet may it be that a person must implore you
> before he can know you?

Encountering God as God is not to take hold of God; it is rather a willingness to be taken hold of by God. St Paul seemed to correct his first, spontaneous attitude in this sentence which describes his search for the fullness of God: 'Not that I have secured it already, not yet reached my goal, but I am still pursuing it in the attempt to take hold of the prize for which Christ Jesus took hold of me.' (Phil 2:12)

God is not 'on tap' to the neutral or curious observer.

This is a reverent readiness to respond, even before we know God; it is commitment to listen even before we receive any communication from God; it is to trust but never to test God, as the opening words of Wisdom tell us: 'Be properly disposed towards the Lord and seek him in simplicity of heart; for he will be found by those who do not put him to the test, revealing himself to those who do not mistrust him.' (Wis 1:1-2) God is not 'on tap' to the neutral or curious observer.

Our very desire to know God is the love of God calling us to trust God, through an open willingness to hear God and to experience the divine love. Let us pray again, slowly and deeply:

> God, you are my God, I pine for you;
> my heart thirsts for you, my body longs for you,
> as a land parched, dreary and waterless.
> So I gaze on you in the sanctuary
> to see your strength and your glory. (Ps 63:1-2)

This must be our constant attitude before God; this is faith. It is far from our stance before a piece of technology, however attractive, advanced or useful.

## Reviewing Chapter Six

Was there anything in this chapter to which you could immediately relate from your own experience?
Were there any new ideas which you found puzzling or worrisome?
Did you find in this chapter anything of benefit to you in your particular role as a Christian?
*You may find it helpful to make a note of any thoughts from this chapter which you would like to remember.*

## Questions for discussion in your group

1. 'The modern person is called to see God's action in modern technology and then to hear the music of God's presence within it.' What is your reaction to that?
2. Our technological instincts tell us to 'use' God. Our faith instincts tell us to 'encounter' God in new ways, with reverence and love. Is this a fair reflection of the struggle to find God in our technological age?

# Chapter 7:
# Responding to the invitation

### *God Is Mystery*

In the language of technology, a mystery is a puzzle which challenges science to solve it. But 'mystery', in the New Testament sense, is something quite different, something so beautiful that it is endlessly rich. A good friendship is such – not a problem to be solved, but something which, when lived with mutual reverence, is ever more enriching for the friends. It is in this way that God is a mystery. God is not someone whom we can never understand, but someone about whom we can never understand enough. In Eamonn Bredin's phrase, a mystery, in this sense, is 'infinitely intelligible.' It is only through God's gift of wisdom that we can gradually encounter the beauty and depth that is God:

> To say that God is mystery is to say that God is infinitely intelligible.

> What human being indeed can know the intentions of
> God?
> And who can comprehend the will of the Lord?
> For the reasoning of mortals is inadequate,
> our attitudes of mind unstable;
> for a perishable body presses down the soul,
> and this tent of clay weighs down the mind with its
> many cares.
> It is hard enough for us to work out what is on earth,
> laborious to know what lies within our reach;
> who, then, can discover what is in the heavens?
> And who could ever have known your will, had you not
> given wisdom
> and sent your Holy Spirit from above? (Wis 9:13-18)

God's gift of wisdom enables us to meet God with our hearts and our whole being, rather than meeting a divine abstraction with our minds. It is our attitude of faith – openness to receive – which turns our experience of

God from a puzzle which challenges our heads, into a friendship which warms our hearts.

*Before the Mystery*

Jesus demonstrated the ideal stance before God; it is described by St Luke: 'People even brought babies to him, for him to touch them; but when the disciples saw this they scolded them. But Jesus called the children to him and said, "Let the little children come to me, and do not stop them; for it is to such as these that the kingdom of God belongs. In truth I tell you, anyone who does not welcome the kingdom of God like a little child will never enter it."'(Lk 18:15-17)

This has nothing to do with childishness; it is childlikeness. A happy child is first of all simple in the deepest meaning of the word, which is 'uncomplicated.' The well-adjusted child is also sincere in lacking all pretence, and spontaneous because he or she lacks all anxious self-consciousness. Although these beautiful qualities are natural gifts of every child, they can of course be destroyed by adults who force them to feel otherwise. But this does not take from the usefulness of the description which Jesus offers us in our search for God. When we allow the technological way of thinking to absorb the whole of our lives, this healthy childlikeness, facilitating our encounter with God, disappears.

'Just at this time, filled with joy by the Holy Spirit, Jesus said, "I bless you, Father, Lord of heaven and earth, for hiding these things from the learned and the clever and revealing them to little children. Yes, Father, for that is what it has pleased you to do."' (Lk 11:21-22)

*Faith – Personal and Varied*

The issues of faith and unbelief have taken a new turn today. The reason is not entirely because of the changes brought by technology; it is also due to the fact that we now look at faith from another angle. In the past, we thought more theoretically about the act of faith and about *what* was believed. We are now inclined to think more about what exactly is *going on* in persons when they say that they believe. Thus the very personal nature of faith, influenced of course by developmental and social factors, is highlighted.

There is a great variety in people's experience of God and all can be genuine and sincere. To put it another way, in their faith, some stress dependence, some commitment, some doing the right thing, some submission, some optimism, some meaning, some searching, some obedience and some endurance. Again, each of these is an aspect of faith, genuine faith, for this person at this time. One may move from faith as dissatisfaction with self, to faith as taking a chance or to faith as expectation or vice versa at any time. Faith is very personal; it is always *your* faith or *my* faith *now.*

Faith is very personal; it is always *your* faith or *my* faith *now.*

People governed more by their heart seem to meet God more easily as father or mother; those who live more from their heads are inclined to encounter God in Jesus offering them meaning, and people who live more in their gut relate best to God as permeating Spirit everywhere.

All this should discourage us from measuring, judging or condemning others whose faith and experience of God seem so different from our own. Many Christians, especially those closely involved in the modern world and under the stress of modern rationalism, can have a rather wintry sort of spirituality but they are faithful to prayer, sacraments and good behaviour. At the other end of the line are those whose faith seems more enthusiastic. Neither of these types is chemically pure, of course, nor may one judge that one is better than the other.

Judging or condemning oneself against the apparently better faith of others is also pointless. We cannot judge the quality of another's belief in God, anymore than we can judge the quality of relationships between friends. Others may appear to have no doubts while you may have many. Be assured again that to have faith is to have doubts. Faith is not a felt certainty; it is a constant, courageous struggle to believe in a living, loving God, sometimes against the immediate evidence. Consider how Jesus must have felt on the cross as he prayed: 'My God, my God, why have you forsaken me?' (Mt 27:47)

The goodness of God is something about which you personally may be deeply aware, but your best friend may be more aware of the greatness of God; you may be struck by the nearness of God, your friend by the incomprehensibility of God; you by God's guidance, your friend by God's authority; you by openness to the Holy Spirit, your friend by openness to serving others; you by membership of the church, your friend by a rather cosy individualistic faith and so on.

Words like 'salvation,' 'prayer,' 'Church,' 'mission,' or 'morality' or even 'God,' will not mean quite the same for different people – nor even for yourself at different times. Living by faith, or *faithing*, leaves plenty of room for everyone's temperament and present experience; we must give others plenty of room too, especially our adolescents.

Let us then have great confidence in the individual temperament which God has given us and live it out faithfully with all its stages of change and of growth. Let us never jump to the conclusion that we or our friends have 'lost the faith' because there is a change in their faith-experience or in our own. This is so important in these times of very rapid change, as so many thinking people are forced to search for a new experience or understanding of God's presence and action in the world.

St Paul offered good advice to his Roman Christians: 'If a person's faith is not strong enough, welcome him all the same, without starting an argument ... if one person keeps certain days as holier than others, and another considers all days to be equally holy, each must be left free to hold his own opinion ... this is why you should never pass judgement on a brother or treat him with contempt, as some of you have done.' (Rom 14:1,5,10)

This is very good advice today in a divided world and in a sometimes divided Church.

*Faith Grows*

In his gospel, St John never mentions the word faith; instead he uses the verb to believe, 72 times. He therefore speaks of *faith-ing*. It is important to remember that there is no such thing as *faith* in the abstract. The word could give the idea that our relationship with God is something static, a substance, something that does not move or live, a thing that can stand by itself without a relationship to anything else.

On the contrary, faith, being lived, is more a verb than a noun; it is something being done, growing with a person. Faith therefore can differ in the same person at different times. St Paul speaks of his acceptance and of his happiness about the growth of faith in the Thessalonian community: 'We must always thank God for you, brothers; quite rightly; because your faith is growing so wonderfully.' (2 Thess 1:3)

What is faith growing towards? It is growing towards closeness, intimacy between ourselves and God; as any good human friendship does. You ask in prayer:

'Create in me a clean heart
renew within me a resolute spirit.' (Ps 51:10)

until you can say more sincerely each day:

'My heart is ready, God,
my heart is ready.' (Ps 57:7)

and then with your whole being you can:

'Act justly,
love tenderly,
and walk humbly with our God.' (cf Mic 6:8)

because you believe and experience the prayer of Jesus:

'May they all be one,
just as, Father, you are in me and I am in you
so that they may be one in us.' (Jn 17:21)

This is a journey, the journey of a lifetime until its end. And it will be the story of many forgiven failures along the way, because God's love is unconditional and forever; it is always merciful love.

## Reviewing Chapter Seven

Was there anything in this chapter to which you could immediately relate from your own experience?
Were there any new ideas which you found puzzling or worrisome?
Did you find in this chapter anything of benefit to you in your particular role as a Christian?
*You may find it helpful to make a note of any thoughts from this chapter which you would like to remember.*

## Questions for discussion in your group

1. What attitudes facilitate an encounter with God in the technological age?
2. In what ways do you find that your faith experience reflects your temperament and your personal story?
3. If faith is many-faceted, what aspects of faith appeal to you personally?

# Chapter 8:
# Salvation now

### *What is God for?*

This seems to be a blasphemous question, but it is not. God is for-*giving* and this is why we were made – so that God's love and God's gifts could be given to us, and that like God we might share them with others. The modern person will have great difficulty believing in a God who, people say, made him or her to 'know, love and serve' that God. There is of course a truth in this, but it is not the deepest truth, not the first truth, as St John reminds us: 'God is love. God's love for us was revealed when God sent into the world his only Son, so that we may have life through him; this is the love I mean: not our love for God but God's love for us...' (1 Jn 4:8b-10)

> Salvation is liberation from everything that oppresses the human person.

As the Irish bishops reminded young people in 1985: 'The only God worth believing in is the God who believed enough in people to die for us. The only God worth living for is the One who calls us to live with him, through a dark faith in this life, and beyond death in face-to-face fullness. The only God worth searching for is the One who searched for us and who still struggles within us in order that we may become more free to love.'

As they say, this is 'the only God worth believing in'; the only God who should ever have been believed in and now the only God that the modern person will believe in anyway.

Jesus tells us why God sent him and what God is for: 'I have come so that they may have life and have it to the full.' (Jn 10:10)

God wants us to be fully alive – physically, emotionally, mentally, socially and spiritually. This is the meaning of the word *Gospel* or *Good News*: 'As the kernel and centre of his Good News, Christ proclaims Salvation, this great gift of God which is: liberation from everything that oppresses the human person, but which is, above all, liberation from Sin and the Evil One, in the joy of knowing God and being known by him, of seeing him and of being given over to him. All this is begun during the life of Christ and definitively accomplished by his death and resurrection. But it must be patiently carried on during the course of history, in order to be realised fully on the day of the final coming of Christ.' (*Evangelii Nuntiandi*, 9)

God wants us to reach full development of our bodies, our affections, our emotions, our appreciation of beauty, our moral life and our relationship with God and with others. This is salvation, redemption, liberation and the fullness of human freedom. The very desire for it within us is the beginning of God's gift calling us to its completion:

> If you make my word your home
> you will indeed be my disciples;
> you will come to learn the truth,
> and the truth will set you free. (Jn 8:31-32)

*Salvation Today*

Properly understood, perhaps *Liberation* best expresses the word *Salvation* for the modern person. Away back in 1927 when modern science was just emerging, an acute observer wrote: 'Science is a match that man has just got alight. He thought he was in a room – in moments of devotion, a temple – and that his light would be reflected from and display walls inscribed with wonderful secrets and pillars carved with philosophical systems wrought into harmony. It is a curious sensation, now that the preliminary sputter is over and the flame burns up clear, to see his hands lit and just a glimpse of himself and the patch he stands on visible, and around him in place of all that human comfort and beauty he anticipated – darkness still.' (H.G.Wells)

Today many modern people wonder if technology's promise of 'progess' has been progress indeed. As postmodernity (i.e. when the benefits of modernity are questioned) is spoken of more frequently, it seems that this wondering may be well worthwhile and that people may need liberation and light as never before.

The human person has always needed salvation, or liberation from such oppressive things as physical, emotional and mental illness, selfishness, poverty of all kinds, needless guilt and fear, loneliness, anger, alienation, loss of meaning, slavery to systems and sin of all kinds. But the technological revolution has brought other oppressions such as meaninglessness, burdensome self-awareness, frustrating expectations, lack of community, consumerism, infidelity, competitiveness, systemic evil and a feeling of being fragmented. It is in these areas that we as modern persons need God's salvation today.

### *Encountering God in Modernity*

For centuries, Christians like ourselves have met God very powerfully in personal prayer, in the Eucharist, the other sacraments, in scripture, in obeying the Word of God and in the beauty of nature around us. Each of these, especially the sacraments of the Church, are strong symbols and channels of God's love for us; they always will be. But in so far as our outlook on life is influenced by technology, we will benefit today from also seeking God in other places.

Firstly, our felt need and desire for God is a deep manifestation of the Divine to us; we can meet God very meaningfully in these.

Now when fidelity has become less frequent in the world, our own friendships and those of others can be signs of God's presence to us also. The fidelity of spouses to difficult partners, of parents to handicapped children and the moral courage of people who suffer greatly, are places of God's presence, if we wish to meet God there.

Our own doubts and our questions about life and its meaning are God's invitation to meet with the Divine and to find those answers in God. So also is our own fidelity in spite of our doubts.

We accept that most of our successes are due to more than personal effort and good luck. We also have to accept that not all of our achievements are fully deserved, and that most of our talents were not earned. 'What have you that you have not received?' (1 Cor 4:7) So often we have experienced an unusual and unexplained power within us, enabling us to survive in very difficult situations. If we are observant of others too, we see what sociologist Peter Berger calls 'signals of transcendence' all round us, in protective mothers, in providing fathers, in devoted children and in the serenity of grandparents; but we must look below the surface to find God in each situation.

The recovered drug addict, the daily faith of the sober alcoholic, the surrender of the person dying with AIDS and the dedication of people in the helping professions, all these bring us face to face with the source of their courageous love because 'God is love and anyone who lives in love lives in God and God in him.' (1 Jn 4:16b) The courage of the blind, the faltering movement of the handicapped and the singlemindedness of the prisoners of conscience remind us of God too. We can meet God in solo parents caring for their children and in the creative dedication of scientists.

God comes to us also in our hunger for love, but especially in our sinfulness, which mediates the constant forgiveness and reconciliation of God into our lives. Each of us has a very personal history of times when we experienced God's presence in love, in power and in mercy, with unusual vividness. Reflecting again on these moments – our salvation history – can be a renewed encounter with the divine.

Our sense of personal responsibility and our willingness to do the right thing without obvious rewards, have their origin in God within us. Even our sense of wonder, or our ability to laugh at ourselves, are passages to the presence of God.

Each new piece of technology reminds us of God's

gift of creativity to people, for which we can thank God and we can pray that its benefits will be shared by all. But because technology is of human making, the human person can never find his or her whole self within it; the person cannot be his or her own product. Technology is a sacrament of God's presence, but it is not God.

Technology is helping selfish people to widen the gap between the poor and the rich in a dreadful way and the same technology in the media brings us all face to face with the poor who are near us or far away.

God is in all people, but has a preferential love for the poor – those on the edge of society. If we seriously wish to have a deep encounter with God today, we do it in the hungry, the lonely, the refugees, the sick, the marginalised and the deprived in any way, whether it be physical or psychological deprivation which they suffer:

'I was hungry... a stranger ... sick ... in prison ... naked ... In truth I tell you, in so far as you did this to one of the least of these brothers of mine, you did it to me.' (Mt 25:35-40)

Finally, the feeling of God's absence, which technology can increase, can be an experience of the Divine presence too as we search for God and remain faithful just the same; this was the experience of the Psalmist:

> Through the night I ponder in my heart,
> as I reflect, my spirit asks this question:
> 'Is the Lord's rejection final?
> Will he never show his favour again?
> Is his faithful love gone for ever?
> His word come to an end for all time?' (Ps 77:6-8)

To sum up, we can meet God in any situation that is true, honourable, upright, pure, lovable, admirable, good or praiseworthy, as St Paul reminds us: 'Let your minds be filled with everything that is true, everything that is honourable, everything that is upright and pure, everything that we love or admire – with whatever is good and praiseworthy.' (Phil 4:8)

### *Verifying the Encounter*

Sometimes the presence of God is accompanied by pleasant feelings, as it might be during prayer, at a liturgy or when enjoying beautiful scenery. But feelings alone do not infallibly indicate an experience of God. When, for instance, you face the struggles of life with courage, keep difficult promises, pray trustfully to a silent God, give to others less well-off, stand in defence of the defenceless or follow your conscience while suffering for it, you are undoubtedly meeting God, but you may not be enjoying it in your feelings; neither was Jesus in the garden of Gethsemane.

You can be sure that your encounter with God is genuine – whether accompanied by a pleasant feeling or not – if it results in your bringing more 'love, joy, peace, patience, kindness, goodness, trustfulness, gentleness and self-control' (Gal 5:22) into the world. If your approach to others always brings them more alive – physically, emotionally, mentally, aesthetically or spiritually – 'so that they may have life and have it to the full' (Jn 10:10), then you are always encountering God, whether you feel it or not.

In Part Five, we shall see how reflective prayer can deepen this encounter.

## Reviewing Chapter Eight

Was there anything in this chapter to which you could immediately relate from your own experience?
Were there any new ideas which you found puzzling or worrisome?
Did you find in this chapter anything of benefit to you in your particular role as a Christian?
*You may find it helpful to make a note of any thoughts from this chapter which you would like to remember.*

## Questions for discussion in your group

1. What do you think real liberation is today?
2. Has it been possible for you to encounter God in your particular technological world?

# *Part Four*
# Morality Now

# Chapter 9:
# Technology: The moral challenge

As we have seen, God can be described as a Creative Lover or a Loving Creator who has made each of us 'in the image and likeness' of this love and this creativity. This is our vocation, our destiny and our fulfilment – to reflect God's creative powers and loving action around us. When we are creative and life-giving, for others and towards the environment, we are God-like, provided that our action is at the same time loving. When my creative action is motivated by love and directed towards giving life to others, or making this a better world, then it is a holy action because it reflects the very life, the very holiness of God.

Our vocation is to reflect God's creative powers and loving action around us.

Parents who choose to give life to a child and lovingly care for it, not only reflect God's creative love but they share it. The anthropologist or historian, who tries to discover more about the human race for its future growth, also continues God's creative love, as does the psychologist, who may help us to understand ourselves for richer and happier living. The painter, plumber, landscaper or cleaner also pass on God's love and life to others, if they choose. So do the dedicated researcher into human genetics and the hardworking engineer or architect planning better cities and homes for all of us.

### *Technology's Pervasiveness*

Over the last fifty years, the creativity of technology has achieved greater prominence than creativity in other ways of life. When we think of creativity today, we are more inclined to think of the aircraft designer than of the artist or the doctor, of the nuclear scientist than of the social worker successfully re-creating

Technology forces choices on us, in which we meet or fail to meet God.

broken families, of the metallurgist than of the mother, and of the computer technician than of the taxi driver patiently performing a work of service for others each day. This biased application of the concept of creativity is to be regretted but it does underline for us that technology influences our attitudes very significantly. To be aware of technology is good in so far as all awareness is good. Its growing influence on our consciousness is simply a fact and its pervading presence is increasingly the human experience today.

It is in this modern experience that we must meet ourselves and so meet God. Of course, as we have seen, we can still meet God in nature, in the sacraments and in prayer, but to bypass the influence of technology on our lives would be to bypass a great part of our human experience today. Every day, every hour, it forces choices on us, in which we meet or fail to meet God.

### *Technology and Choice*

Technology calls for a constant sense of responsibility and effective choice.

'Nearly every aspect of modern life in the Western world has been deeply affected by technology. The changes continue on an almost daily basis: travel, information-flow, education, construction, cooking, business, medicine and so on. I have no precise idea how this relates to moral theology, but one cannot avoid the nagging suspicion that it may re-inforce some deeply-embedded Western and American value priorities – efficiency and comfort. If these are indeed the values that shape our perspectives, it should be fairly clear that we are knee-deep in danger that they will corrosively affect our judgements of the morally right and wrong, and more generally the priority of values.' (Richard McCormick SJ, in *Theological Studies*, March 1989.)

It is clearly possible to use or misuse technology, to have it serve us or enslave us. Our cars can make us mobile to the extent of destroying reflectiveness or they can give us more time for prayer. Air travel can distract, exhaust or refresh us. Kitchen mod-cons can give us time to meditate or to mess up our lives, and television can fill our minds with useful or useless information.

Clearly, technology puts constant choices before us. It is often easier to make selfish and shortsighted choices than wise and enriching ones. Technology, with its vast potential for good or evil, calls for a constant sense of responsibility and effective choice. When, for instance, must we simplify our lifestyles in order to slow down technology's invasion of the environment?

Not to make the responsible choice is to make the irresponsible one.

This call for responsible attitudes and action cannot be sidestepped; it cannot be avoided. Not to make the responsible choice is to make the irresponsible one. Not to choose to oppose injustice is to choose to be unjust; not to choose some time for reflection each day is to choose passivity and to drift. Not to resist the newest and latest is to become a trapped consumer, and not to react critically to advertisements is to accept their influence. Not to make a choice is to allow a choice to be made for us by those who may not be concerned about our welfare.

This need for constant choice, in the face of technology's readiness to serve instinctual needs instantly, becomes particularly important for parents. Their decisions can have long-lasting effects on children, who can grow up discerning and disciplined or gripped by the gadgetry of the moment. The poor, aged, lonely, imprisoned, ill or handicapped will be unnoticed and untouched if technology's *use-to-me* language permeates and paganises our Christian existence. Again, the making of responsible choices – in each of which we meet God – is urgent.

Because technology, in its good and evil results, travels widely and has global influence, it is an instrument about which important choices have to be made. Such choices include the use and abuse of nuclear power, environmental improvement or harm, economic sharing or isolation of some nations, political participation or manipulation of whole populations, compassionate migration or the merciless movement of refugees. Here we go beyond responsibility for our personal lives and those who live near us. In some distant but very real way, we must do what we can for the fifteen million refugees, the many prisoners of conscience, the 40,000 children dying quietly of malnutrition each day, the millions denied a voice in their own destiny, and speak against the expenditure of about $900 billion on arms each year. The technology of radio and television bring these human facts before us constantly and they demand at least a moral attitude towards them on our part.

Advances in technology can certainly be a fulfilment of God's command in Genesis to 'subdue the earth' and to 'rule over all created things.' (*Eucharistic Prayer 4*) God's creativity in the human person is expressed and manifested in every advance of human knowledge. But has all this technological creativity been loving? Is it always lovingly motivated? Is it used to transmit life and love to ourselves, to others and to the environment? What is my attitude to, and use of, technology in my life? These are the truly human questions, the deep questions. It is in facing the last one particularly, that I meet myself morally.

### *Choice – The Human Act*

Animals can act, can create; the beaver's dam is a marvel of creativity. But the animal's activity is motivated by instinct, not by free choice. It is not the animal's nature to reflect on and choose between alternatives. The animal cannot consciously weigh up the rightness or wrongness of choices before it; this is the human privilege. In fact it is at this moment of considered choice, reflected-upon action, that the human person is most fully human. In every choice or non-choice, a person expresses his or her very centre, his or her total self. Here, non-choice is a

> A constant failure to choose to love leads to making a final choice of not loving God for eternity.

choice; if I do not choose to do the right thing, I automatically choose not to do it. In practice, this is choosing to do the wrong thing.

To be human is to choose. Every moment of human life faces us with a choice or non-choice and life itself is ultimately one big choice, the sum of many smaller ones. A constant failure to choose to love places me in the situation of having made a final choice of not loving God for eternity. It is choice which gives value to every act; it is choice which makes it a human act, not the instinctual reaction of an animal. When I choose I create or disintegrate myself in some way. After I do the right thing by an act of honesty, generosity, fidelity, justice, kindness or courage, I am a more integrated and mature person, but when I choose immorally, I am less so.

My most human, most personal, most authentic and deepest moment is when I choose to act lovingly. It is at this precious moment that I meet myself most fully and continue to develop myself most authentically. It is when I choose to act unjustly, dishonestly, with cowardice or with self-concern only, that I become less human and less whole. Today, technology tends to favour social forces which press for passivity and conformity. Anonymity and marginalisation reduce the likelihood of personal decision to a minimum, making choice and commitment stand unsupported. As we saw in Part Two, the individual has emerged from the group to freedom but also to isolation, making moral decisions more difficult than ever before.

> Technology tends to favour passivity and conformity.

At the same time, never was moral decision more necessary than now as modernity moves along, morally neutral, directionless and unpredictable. An unwise person is one who has acquired knowledge beyond his or her ability to think, but a still greater tragedy is a person equipped beyond his or her wisdom to decide. Piloting a jet without navigational knowledge would be dangerous. Technology tends to equip all of us beyond our ability to choose wisely, unless we are very thoughtful and disciplined. Its language – now is better than later, bigger is better than smaller, more is better than less, faster is better than slower, yes is better than no, and my interests better than those of others – can undermine deep moral choices and eliminate all disciplined decisions in our lives. It is for this reason that technology calls us to deeper humanness and a purified faith.

## Reviewing Chapter Nine

Was there anything in this chapter to which you could immediately relate from your own experience?
Were there any new ideas which you found puzzling or worrisome?
Did you find in this chapter anything of benefit to you in your particular role as a Christian?
*You may find it helpful to make a note of any thoughts from this chapter which you would like to remember.*

## Questions for discussion in your group

1. The world of technology that surounds us, and that makes up a great part of our daily experience, puts an onus on us to make positive choices. In what ways?
2. What are the consequences of not making choices in a technological society?
3. The deeper values can only be grasped in our technological age by those willing to make active choices and active decisions. Comment.
4. Can technology be for our salvation?

# Chapter 10: Conscience and morality

*Serious Choices*

'Everything now depends on man. Immense power of destruction is given into his hand, and the question is whether he can resist the will to use it and can temper his will with the spirit of love and wisdom. He will hardly be capable of doing so on his own unaided resources. He needs the help of an advocate in heaven ... who brings the healing and making-whole of the hitherto fragmentary man.' (Jung, *Answer to Job* p. 636)

'So much is at stake and so much depends on the psychological constitution of modern man. Is he capable of resisting the temptation to use his power for the purpose of staging a world conflagration? Is he conscious of the path he is treading and what the conclusions are that must be drawn from the present world situation and his own psychic situation? Does he realise what lies in store should this catastrophe ever befall him? And finally does the individual know that he is the makeweight that tips the scales? ... The individual human being, that infinitesimal unit on whom a world depends.'
(Jung, *The Undiscovered Self* pp.112-113)

'The only thing that really matters now is whether man can climb up to a higher moral level, to a higher plane of consciousness, in order to be equal to the superhuman powers which ... have played into his hands. But he can make no progress with himself unless he becomes very much better acquainted with his own nature. Unfortunately, a terrifying ignorance prevails in this respect, and an equally great aversion to increasing the knowledge of his intrinsic character.' (Jung, *Answer to Job*, p.638)

*Conscience*

Jung speaks of 'The spirit of love and wisdom,' of 'an advocate in heaven,' of 'a higher moral level,' of 'a higher plane of consciousness,' of becoming 'much better acquainted with his own nature,' of 'increasing the knowledge of his intrinsic character' and of 'losing the life-preserving myth of the inner man which Christianity has treasured up for him.' It would not be easy now to understand the precise meaning of all these Jungian phrases, but they all have this in common: they speak of an innermost self, our centre, of the place in us where we are most morally ourselves – our conscience.

Conscience is our innermost self, our centre, the place in us where we are most morally ourselves.

To survive and grow in humanness and holiness today, each of us will have to return to our centre, the place where we most meet God and from which we find the moral energy to meet modernity. Cultural pressures and pseudo authorities tell us what to think and what to do today, and so it is that our moral faculty must be developed as never before. The modern person has high levels of anxiety about self and survival, is constantly unfulfilled because of rising expectations and is told to consume to the point of exhaustion. This avalanche of conflicting messages can be dealt with only by a mature conscience, which is another word for a centred, moral, self.

Despite the felt need to get together for mutual support, as modern persons we have great hesitations about common purpose and we fear commitment to others. The psychoanalyst, Erickson, described the intimacy each one longs for as, 'the capacity to commit oneself to concrete affiliations and partnerships and to develop ethical strength to abide by such commitments, even though they may call for significant sacrifice and compromise.' Without a well-developed conscience, this is impossible today because we are constantly being urged to become more self-centred. An even less desirable aspect of this unreadiness for intimacy is the modern person's experience of distrust, competitiveness and fragmentedness – which again, only the integrity of a personal value system and mature conscience will heal.

*Moral Maturity*

There is a parallel here with physical fitness; our muscles can be flexible or flabby. In the same way our moral muscles, which enable us to recognise, choose and do the best thing, can be strong or weak. From a Christian point of view, we can be more open or less open to do God's will in our lives and more or less 'moulded to the pattern of his Son.' (Rom 8: 29b)

When we say that a person is morally mature, we are saying a great deal, not merely about the person's conduct, but about the person's entire way of looking at life. Morality is the whole person, made up of a more or less permanent attitude, and of positions taken more or less consistently. We are speaking even about their motives and the pattern of their day to day behaviour. People's morality is their deep and fairly permanent stance towards themselves and others – and towards God, if they have faith.

Morality is the whole person, made up of a more or less permanent attitude, and of positions taken more or less consistently.

For the Christian, morality expresses the mystery of a loving God, dealing with us and having a destiny for us. It concerns the sheer wonder of our being as we respond in freedom to God's invitation. Morality is so much more than a measure of behaviour; it is the lived out experience of Jesus' prayer: 'May they all be one, just as, Father, you are in me and I am in you, so that they also may be one in us ... With me in them and you in me, may they be so perfected in unity that the world will recognise that it was you who sent me and that you have loved them as you loved me.' (Jn 17:21-23) Technology has even less to say about this than it has about a perfect friendship.

To grow in moral maturity, we must recognise our bias towards evil and our weakness in the face of temptation. We must also be willing to accept moral education and guidance and be open to the Holy Spirit. It is also essential that we be open to the constant death to our own selfishness which this will bring, as Jesus said: 'If anyone wants to be a follower of mine, let him renounce himself and take up his cross every day and follow me.' (Lk 9:23) Moral growth entails constant decisions to act morally.

*Moral Complexities Today*

Among people touched by technology, moral maturity has entered a new phase. To be free for moral decisions in a modern city is not the same as being ready for such decisions in rural life fifty years ago. Technology has rendered life immensely complex, as it offers each of us endless meanings and possible behaviours. Many people today are faced with making moral decisions, such as working for a company which exploits poor countries' workers, refusing promotion for the sake of family life, taking non-violent action for social justice, increasing the size of one's family, entering or leaving politics for upright reasons, or living a simpler lifestyle. These decisions are being made in a very complex and sometimes confusing environment and could result in a modern but very real experience of crucifixion.

## Reviewing Chapter Ten

Was there anything in this chapter to which you could immediately relate from your own experience?
Were there any new ideas which you found puzzling or worrisome?
Did you find in this chapter anything of benefit to you in your particular role as a Christian?
***You may find it helpful to make a note of any thoughts from this chapter which you would like to remember.***

## Questions for discussion in your group

1. Conscience has to be sharp, alert and used to making choices. How do we inform our conscience?
2. Discuss some of the moral complexities which you have experienced.

# Chapter 11: Living Christian morality

Unlike earlier times, we can no longer decide what to do by simply applying clear, universal norms even though we still respect them. The areas where norms alone cannot guide us today, in personal, inter-personal and political life, are increasing. How to invest money or choose a career? What party to join or how to become responsibly informed on disarmament? How to approach a morally right and humanly necessary family planning? Whether to conceive a baby with the help of medical technology? In such matters, while we continue to respect and consult Church guidance, the flood of information and constant changing of circumstances make moral decisions very difficult.

> The basis of christian morality is twofold: to believe in God's love for us and to permit that love to pass through us to others.

While Christ did not offer a moral system as such, he preached the reign of God's goodness and love holding sway over our lives. He did not just leave us with the broad guidelines of the ten commandments telling us to love God and our neighbour with our whole being. He went further and deeper offering us a new commandment: 'Love one another, as I have loved you.' (Jn 15:12) It was expressed by St John in this way: 'His commandment is this, that we should believe in the name of his Son Jesus Christ and that we should love each other.' (1 Jn 3:23)

The basis of Christian morality is thus twofold: to believe in God's love for us through Christ and to permit that love to pass through us to others by the power of the Spirit. 'Because the love of God has been poured into our hearts by the Holy Spirit which has been given to us.' (Rom 5:5)

Thus Christian morality, like all morality, calls for self-transcendence. Beyond merely human morality, it adds a deeper insight, a stronger motivation and a consciousness of the Spirit's power. The limitlessness of moral courage is given to us in the life of Jesus: 'This is the proof of love, that he laid down his life for us and we too ought to lay down our lives for our brothers.' (1 Jn 3:16)

Once again, we do not find detailed moral guidance either in the life of Jesus nor in other parts of the Scriptures. For instance, there is no explicit New Testament commandment to love God. The bible offers us only a unique self-understanding, a specific context for understanding the moral life and, of course, the strongest motivation for being moral. The beatitudes (Mt 5 & 6) give us moral attitudes which are much more than a programme of behaviour.

*Church Guidance*

To the leaders of his church, Jesus said: 'As the Father sent me, so I am sending you.' (Jn 20:21) 'Go, therefore, make disciples of all nations – and teach them to observe all the commands I gave you, and look, I am with you always; yes, to the end of time.' (Mt 28:19-20).

The church calls the individual Christian to a humble openness before its moral guidance.

This is not a carte blanche for arbitrary authoritarianism by church leadership, but on it is built the doctrine that Christ, who left behind no writing, did leave behind a tradition and teaching body – the church. It has authority by virtue of him who made it custodian of this tradition, which it believes is humankind's most precious treasure. Like any community destined to endure, the church has a core of settled convictions and some authority charged with the task of nurturing, defending and transmitting those convictions. Although not without the possibility of error and change in non-essentials, the church's doctrinal teachings and moral guidelines flow from these convictions.

Timothy, for instance, used this moral guidance saying: '...but in case I should be delayed, I want you to know how people ought to behave in God's household –

that is, the church of the living God, pillar and support of the truth.' (Tim 3:15) St Paul reminded Timothy about the church's obligation to transmit, nurture and defend God's message: 'Before God and before Christ Jesus, who is to be judge of the living and the dead, I charge you ... to proclaim the message and, welcome or unwelcome, insist on it. Refute falsehood, correct error, give encouragement – but do all with patience and with care to instruct.' (2 Tim 4:1-2)

Popes and bishops have done similarly since then, in their attempts to help people form their consciences and guide their behaviour. However, principles and laws do not dispense us from the conscientious duty to apply them in the circumstances of our lives. One is not justified merely by obeying a law; it is conscience which must apply principles and laws in each case. And, of course, there is the obligation to have our conscience as well informed and as unbiased as we can.

As we have seen, technology has usefully taught us to ask questions and to question authority, while it may also have made its contribution to an age of relentless materialism and instant gratification. But now there appears to be a quickening sense that humankind is made for something finer and needs some fixity in fundamental beliefs. Church leaders have the burdensome privilege of offering this, if they are true to their vocation. That they have not always done so well, and that they have not always been listened to even when they did, is a matter of very clear history.

### *Personal Responsibility*

Vatican II reminds us that the laity 'should not consider that their pastors always have the expertise needed to provide a concrete and ready answer to every problem which arises, even the most serious ones, or that this is their mission.' (GS 43) It also reminds us that 'all the faithful, clerical as well as lay, have a just freedom of enquiry, of

In the final analysis, conscience is inviolable.

thought and of humble and courageous expression in those matters in which they enjoy competence.' (GS 62) Yet, despite the human limitations of its leadership, the church's promised guidance by the Holy Spirit, its clear concern to protect human dignity, and its accumulated wisdom of the centuries, calls the individual Christian to a humble openness before its moral guidance.

Moral maturity means the courage to accept greater freedom but also greater responsibility. This maturity is a somewhat solitary business but it must be supported by prayer for God's guidance and an openness to the traditions of the church community. St Paul reminds us: 'After all, brothers, you were called to be free; do not use your freedom as an opening for self-indulgence.' (Gal 5:13)

Thus, to act contrary to church moral guidance may or may not be sinful, as the Vatican Department for the Clergy wrote on the matter of family planning, in 1971: 'Particular circumstances surrounding an objectively evil human act, while they cannot make it objectively virtuous, can make it inculpable, diminished in guilt or subjectively defensible ... in the final analysis, conscience is inviolable as the traditional moral teaching of the church holds.' (*L'Osservatore Romano* 20/5/71) St John says basically the same thing: 'My dear people, if we cannot be condemned by our own conscience, we need not be afraid in God's presence.' (1 Jn 3:21)

Referring to the same matter, Bishop Murphy-O'Connor wrote: 'The encyclical does not condemn those who do not or cannot always respond to its invitation. Married people who practise artificial birth control for good motives are judged by the ordinary norms of Catholic pastoral theology. Sometimes the practice may be lightly sinful, sometimes no sin at all; rarely, if ever, should it be an obstacle to the reception of Holy Communion. Indeed, how can the faithful begin to understand the prophetic wisdom of the document if they are not nourished by the Body of the Lord?' (*The Tablet*, 13/10/84)

While every Christian listens to church counsel, in

the final analysis he or she is responsible before God for personal moral choices and must accept the risk that accompanies that maturity. Today, when so many opinions and ideologies barrage the human person, each of us must find his or her own centre – conscience – where God speaks. All church guidance must be directed towards helping this, as St Paul's was to Timothy: 'The final goal at which this instruction aims is love, issuing from a pure heart, a clear conscience and a sincere faith ... these are the instructions that I am giving you, so that in their light you may fight like a good soldier with faith and good conscience for your weapon. Some people have put conscience aside and wrecked their faith in consequence.' (1 Tim 1:5,18,19)

It is important to remember that a long habit of not acting as one believes, leads eventually to believing as one acts.

*Moral Disintegration*

The benefits of technology are many and obvious. It has been and continues to be used for human betterment in almost endless ways, but built into each new piece of technology there is an empty pilot's seat, inviting direction on the inevitable motion which it possesses. Moving from metaphor to fact, we quote Charles Lindbergh, who piloted the first solo transatlantic flight in 1927: 'I have felt the godlike power man derives from his machines ... the immortal viewpoint of the higher air ... But I have seen the science I worshipped and the aircraft I loved destroying the civilisation I expected them to serve ... To progress, even to survive, we must learn to apply the truths of God to the direction of our science.'

The human person must choose to pilot or be piloted by technology.

Technology has come a long way since 1927; it is no longer a matter of machines, but of the human person who must choose to pilot or be piloted by the technology he or she has invented. Human inventions now have the potential to put people's focus outside themselves unless we individually choose otherwise; they tend to disintegrate rather than integrate our lives. The higher forms of human experience like truth, goodness, beauty and faith are not its concern. One might say that technology knows the cost of everything, but the value of nothing.

Technology sells itself smoothly as it appeals to power, prestige and possessiveness. These instincts, when excessively catered to, break up relationships and communities through the competitiveness which underlies them. For good or evil, technology favours speed and mobility and thus tends to eliminate time for reflection unless this is consciously chosen. Finally, because it encourages questions and change, it can easily undermine the individual's confidence in his or her values and perceptions. It is the pilot who decides whether these less-beneficial results of technology will arrive.

*Moral Integration*

The pilot is each human person, but he or she is without navigational aids unless seated at his or her own centre – conscience – where God is encountered most fully. It is in meeting oneself at one's deep centre, where decisions are made to do the right thing, that God's creative love is fully active. When a choice is made to transcend one's self-interest for a higher goal, the human person is most human, most holy and most God-like. It is at this moment that one obeys God's appeal to us through Paul to the Philippian community: 'Let your minds be filled with everything that is true, everything that is honourable, everything that is upright and pure, everything that we love and admire, with whatever is good and praiseworthy.' (Phil 4:8)

Where the Spirit of the Lord is, there is freedom.

It is also the moment of deepest worship, without which external worship is mere ritual: 'I urge you, then, brothers, remembering the mercies of God, to offer your bodies as a living sacrifice, dedicated and acceptable to God; that is the kind of worship for you as sensible people.

Do not model your behaviour on the contemporary world, but let the renewing of your minds transform you, so that you may discern for yourselves what is the will of God – what is good, acceptable and mature.' (Rom 12:1-2)

When we act conscientiously, we overcome even our own possible slavery to instinct. We should try to be aware that it is by the power of God's Spirit we achieve this: 'You, however, live not by your natural inclinations, but by the Spirit, since the Spirit of God has made a home in you.' (Rom 8:9) 'And where the Spirit of the Lord is, there is freedom.' (2 Cor 3:17)

Jesus expressed this moment of his total freedom when he said: 'The Father loves me, because I lay down my life in order to take it up again. No one takes it from me; I lay it down of my own free will ... ' (Jn 10:17-18)

This moment when the individual descends into his or her own centre – concerning small or major issues – is the maximum moment of God-filled discernment. It is the moment of discipleship because it is the moment of disciplined spiritual energy. It is the moment of greatest human integration, when one chooses to live by one's own deepest authority, because one authorises growth in personal godliness. And when we learn to reflect on this centredness, it is greater still.

It is not a selfish moment, because the decision to do what is right is a moment of true self-transcendent freedom, above the painless surrender to self and instinct. It is freedom *from* self in order to be free *for* others. It is a religious act even if we are not aware of it.

'For the great sacrifice to God is this – that peace and brotherly concord exist between us and that we be a people united in the unity of the Father, the Son and the Holy Spirit.' (St Cyprian's commentary on *The Lord's Prayer*)

When we feel the internal pain, or experience the external persecution which can so often accompany conscientious decisions, we know that this was the experience of Jesus, especially in Gethsemane and on Calvary. St

Paul asks and answers the human question: 'So I find this rule: that for me, where I want to do nothing but good, evil is close at my side. In my inmost self I dearly love God's law, but I see that acting on my body there is a different law which battles against the law of my mind. So I am brought to be a prisoner of the law of sin which lives inside my body. What a wretched man I am! Who will rescue me from this body doomed to death? God – thanks be to him – through Jesus Christ our Lord.' (Rom 7:21-25)

It is from this centre where conscientious decisions are made, that the modern Christian can challenge and pilot technology towards the benefits God meant it to produce for humankind. In Part Five, we will consider the lived fruits of this centred moment.

## Reviewing Chapter Eleven

Was there anything in this chapter to which you could immediately relate from your own experience?
Were there any new ideas which you found puzzling or worrisome?
Did you find in this chapter anything of benefit to you in your particular role as a Christian?
*You may find it helpful to make a note of any thoughts from this chapter which you would like to remember.*

## Questions for discussion in your group

1. Discuss some instances of moral courage today.
2. Where do you yourself draw your moral guidance from?
3. How does the church help you personally in coming to moral decisions?
4. What difficulties do you experience in applying your moral values in today's technological world?
5. Did you ever feel alone in making a moral decision?
6. Who do you think the modern saints are?

# *Part Five*
# Living Faith Now

# Chapter 12:
# A new presence of God

As technology changes people, it challenges us to find new ways in which to express and nourish our faith. Like our love for our friends, faith can never be disassociated from how we express it. Unless we express our faith in a way that is level with life as we live it, it will become a formula for Sunday religious behaviour disconnected from the rest of the week, or we will reduce God to magic and make-believe.

Like our love for our friends, faith can never be disassociated from how we express it.

Back in 1950, a famous historian wrote, 'Men today are divided between those who have kept their spiritual roots and lost their contact with the existing order of society, and those who have preserved their social contacts and lost their spiritual ones.' (Christopher Dawson) Either can happen to any of us today.

Flowers, trees and the human organism survive great changes in temperature, moisture content and wind strength, because they adapt without losing their unique life-force or identity. Any organism which fails to face up to change, which refuses to change, becomes a fossil. This is true of all secular and religious organisations as well. For this reason, highly stratified groups, hierarchical organisations, and social or religious castes, could have a built-in death-wish if they set their faces against adaptation and change today. Pope John XXIII explained his decision to call the Second Vatican Council by saying that he did not wish the church to become a museum. That is also why scholars now recognise that the place of theology is life, not the library.

If we now wish to grow in our faith life (or faithing) – and it must grow if it is to survive – then each of us needs to reflect deeply on our experience of God and learn to express it in ways that are new.

*Feeling Your Way Towards God*

When St Paul went to Greece, he collided with a new and much more secularised culture than he had in Palestine. 'His whole soul was revolted at the sight of a city given over to idolatry.' (Acts 17:16) These people did not have culture and common faith supporting each other as the Israelites had. It was a situation somewhat like the modern one, where religious people no longer have cultural support for their values and way of life. Paul could not just quote scripture to these people; he had to speak to them from where they were. He could not even mention Jesus Christ to them; he had to start farther back. As modern persons, we may have to do the same – even in our own lives. He began by quoting from two of their own pagan poets:

> Instead of relying on isolated religious experience, we must learn to find the religiousness of *all* experience.

'And he (God) did this so that they might seek the deity and, by feeling their way towards him, might succeed in finding him; and indeed he is not far from any of us, since it is in him that we live, move and exist, as indeed your own writers have said: "We are his children."' (Acts 17:27-28)

Each of us has moments of high encounter with God, perhaps in the Sacraments, in praying the scriptures, making love to a spouse or enjoying a sunset, but these are comparatively rare; they don't happen every day. It is essential that we get in contact with the God in whom 'we live, move and exist.'

Instead of relying on isolated religious experience, we must learn to find the religiousness of *all* experience. Notice that St Paul is not speaking about a magical, hey-presto presence of God, but of our 'feeling' our way towards him, since 'he is not far from any of us.' In this way our faith is not confined to holy days, holy places and holy events, since every day, place and event has a holy presence in its depths: 'Through him (God's Word) all things came to be, not one thing had its being but through him. All that came to be had life in him.' (Col 3:11)

Only the person who has discovered the presence of God's Spirit within can turn outwards towards a transcendant God. 'The Spirit explores the depths of everything, even the depths of God.' (1 Cor 2:10)

This means establishing a constant connection between God in the depth of us and the same God who comes to us. Poetically, it could be expressed another way:

Earth is crammed with heaven
and every common bush afire with God,
but only those who see,
take off their shoes.
The rest sit round and pick blackberries.
(Elizabeth Browning)

The technological mind is functional, concentrating on the 'useful'; it picks the blackberries and misses the fire within. We must take off our shoes to meet God.

When we develop an openness to mystery, as described in Part Four, the willingness to see what everyone else sees but more deeply, then we meet God everywhere. For many years of his life, St Augustine considered material things somehow unholy, but when he met God more he wrote: 'I saw your unchangeable light shining over the eye of my soul ... I thought about those things which are less than you ... And it became clear to me that corruptible things are good ... And I say that 'those other things' owe their being to you and that all finite things are in you; but in a different manner, being in you not as in a place, but because you are and hold all things in the hand of your Truth.' (*Confessions* 7:10-12,15)

In more recent years, a famous priest palaeontologist prayed: 'Give me to recognise in other men, Lord God, the radiance of your own face. The invisible light of your eyes, shining in the face of things has already driven me into undertaking the work I had to do and into facing the difficulties I had to overcome ... May the Risen Christ keep me young for God's greater glory – young, that is, optimistic, active, smiling, perceptive.' (Teilhard de Chardin)

Dietrich Bonhoeffer, the modern Lutheran martyr, says that unless we see the mysteries below the surface of life, we are not seeing reality. To see a tree, without some awareness of its roots in the dark earth, is a failure to see the 'heart' of the tree; to forget that all human life comes from the darkness of the womb is to miss much of what is human.

Look around you and think of the great gifts of modern technology, while you pray this prayer:

God our Father,
open our eyes to see your hand at work
in the splendour of creation,
in the beauty of human life.
Touched by your hand, our world is holy.
Help us to cherish the gifts that surround us,
to share your blessing with our brothers and sisters
and to experience the joy of life in your presence.
(17th Sunday in Ordinary Time)

Faith for today begins with a simple willingness to say this kind of prayer and mean it, and then to 'feel' your way towards the God in whom we 'live, move and exist.'

## Reviewing Chapter Twelve

Was there anything in this chapter to which you could immediately relate from your own experience?
Were there any new ideas which you found puzzling or worrisome?
Did you find in this chapter anything of benefit to you in your particular role as a Christian?
*You may find it helpful to make a note of any thoughts from this chapter which you would like to remember.*

## Questions for discussion in your group

1. How do you find God's presence in the creations of technology?
2. Do you ever have a moment of encounter with God in the surroundings of technology?
3. Are you losing faith in God?

# Chapter 13: A personal faith

Faith can no longer be a formula, a list of things we believe in, a creed recited casually on a Sunday, nor a ritual, however well performed. Nor can it be something we accept because those around us do. The modern world has taken away the scaffolding and the building must have its own internal support. Not only has the scaffolding been moved but the testing winds of modernity have grown in velocity. Faith must be deeply owned today.

The modern world has taken away the scaffolding and the building must have its own internal support.

Technology tends to throw in new questions, to isolate the individual, and to force a search for meaning within the self. It will also call for a personal and adult conscience because responsible decisions will have to be made without detailed guidelines being available.

St Paul put the central question about personal and deep faith: 'Examine yourselves to make sure you are really in the faith; test yourselves. Do you acknowledge that Jesus Christ is really in you? If not, you have failed the test.' (2 Cor 13:5)

Although, as we saw in Part Three, for the person of faith all life is a prayer, it has always been necessary to have time for prayer away from the market-place of life. This is more necessary than ever today. The modern Christian needs time to recognise and to accept ever more deeply God's loving presence and action is his or her life.

'All who are guided by the Spirit of God are sons of God; for what you received was not the spirit of slavery to bring you back into fear, you received the spirit of adoption, enabling us to cry out, 'Abba, Father!' The Spirit himself joins with our spirit to bear witness that we are children of God. And if we are children, then we are heirs, heirs of God and joint-heirs with Christ, provided that we share his suffering, so as to share his glory.' (Rom 8:14-17)

*Praying*

Then, with the Holy Spirit within us, and confidently through that Spirit, we must hold regular conversations with God – listening and speaking, as the Spirit moves us. This is prayer as we have always known it. Mantra prayer too can be a healthy antidote to the hurried heartbeat of modern people.

> It seems necessary to practice the prayer of searching and of slow reflection.

However, today, because of the apparent absence of the sacred, it seems very necessary to practice another kind of prayer – the prayer of searching and of slow reflection. This is basically a decision to be alone for some time regularly, in order to ponder how God met you and how you responded, or failed to respond, in your every day experiences. It is, as it were, a pre-view of your time ahead and a replay of the time gone by from God's point of view.

Ideally this is done at the beginning and at the end of each day. It is a thinking-over, a pondering on events, people, decisions which will come or have come our way during the day. When we do this regularly, it will sharpen the eyesight of our faith, to recognise and listen to God's message in the very ordinariness of daily existence. From this experience we will naturally respond to God in gratitude, in need, in frustration, in wonder, in regret or in hope – but in depth.

It can even lead to expressing disappointment to God as holy people have done for centuries:

> 'My God, I call by day but you do not answer,
> at night, but I find no respite.' (Ps 10:1)
> 'Why, Yahweh, do you keep so distant,
> stay hidden in times of trouble?' (Ps 10:1)

Praying from the scriptures or other writings will always help some; the psalms, for instance, can sometimes express our deepest thoughts accurately. But unless the modern person practices the prayer of reflection, his or her life can easily fall into two parts – one sacred or religious and the other secular or mundane. It is prayer of reflection which unites these and makes for the integration of life which technology tends to disintegrate. This prayer has the great advantage that one starts from life-experience and penetrates to its depths, while technology tends to hurry us along in a shallow way from one experience to the next. It also ensures that we do not drop out into abstract contemplation, or burn out through ceaseless activity.

### *A Supported Faith*

Modern life springs from, and promotes, the emergence of the individual from the group. Often this has good results, but it can also have some not-so-obviously-good ones, as each of us today feels less social support than our parents did. Technology favours common purpose only for its utility, not for its help to people. So it is that, more than ever, the person today needs a community of common faith and love, lest individual values die from isolation.

> Today, more than ever, we need a community of common faith and love.

As conflict and competition increase, so does the individual's need for closeness and simple human support. As Christians, we need this human support but our precious experience of God's presence also needs affirmation. Even St Paul told his Roman friends how he and they needed this: 'I am longing to see you so that I may convey to you some spiritual gift that will be of lasting strength, or rather that we may be strengthened together through our mutual faith, yours and mine.' (Rom 1:11-12)

This need for explicit mutual support is a constant theme of the early Church: 'So give encouragement to each other, and keep strengthening one another, as you already do.' (1 Thess 5:11) 'Teach each other and advise each other in all wisdom.' (Col 3:16) 'When there are some who have doubts, reassure them; when there are some to be saved from the fire, pull them out.' (Jude 23a) 'Let us be concerned for each other, to stir a response in love and good works.' (Heb 10:24)

It is nearly impossible to develop a living faith today without belonging to a group or community which clearly shares that faith. It is not enough to have church services together because, of their nature, they do not allow for spontaneous expressions of faith and mutual support. If I live alone (i.e. uninvolved), whose feet will I wash? Each of us today needs to know that others near us believe, to hear them say it in prayer or in testimony, and to see it in action. And for the discernment before important decisions, which come upon us so quickly today, we need the collective wisdom of such a faith-community as well.

*An Involved Faith*

We all know the story of Dives and Lazarus (Lk 16:19-31) and we feel sure that if Lazarus were outside our door during a meal, we would readily share with him. We know too that St James is talking Christian sense here: 'Take the case, my brothers, of someone who has never done a single good act but claims that he has faith. Will that faith save him? If one of the brothers or one of the sisters is in need of clothes and has not enough food to live on, and one of you says to them, 'I wish you well; keep yourself warm and eat plenty,' without giving them these bare necessities of life, then what good is that? Faith is like that; if good works do not go with it, it is quite dead.' (Jas 2:14-17)

> Action for justice seems to be such an important expression of faith today.

But, thanks to the technology of television, we can now see Lazarus in the millions who are deprived of food, eduation, health, housing and leisure, sometimes by the power-hungry and money-seekers in our own country or in others. Corrupt politicians and military generals are using technology to enslave and impoverish millions. We not only know and see the marginalisation, oppression and deprivation of these people, but, if we want to, we can know the causes of it. Ignorance of either the facts or the causes puts us with Dives who did not look out his window. And, in so far as we own or use more than we need, we dine with Dives too. 'I was hungry and you never gave me food ... a stranger and you never made me welcome ... naked and you never clothed me ... I tell you solemnly, in so far as you neglected to do it to one of the least of these, you neglected to do it to me.' (cf Mt 25:42-46)

If in any way we have fallen for the message of modernity, that more is always better than less, we will benefit from these words of St Basil, in the fourth century: 'The bread you do not use is the bread of the hungry; the garment hanging in your wardrobe is the garment of him who is naked; the shoes you do not wear are the shoes of one who is bare-foot; the money you keep locked away is the money of the poor; the acts of charity you do not perform are so many injustices you commit.'

Not to possess more than we need is an important expression of faith today, when consumerism causes so much waste and deprivation. Then, sharing what we have, or giving it away, even when it is useful to us, is another normal expression of faith. But it is action for justice which seems to be such an important expression of faith today. This action either speaks against or challenges systematic evil. Of course each person must decide in conscience the level of involvement to which he or she feels called. And, as well as sharing what we have and acting for justice, we can of course tell God about our desire for universal justice in prayer.

To be a Christian and a member of the church today is to accept and act on these words from Vatican II: 'The joys and hopes, the grief and anxieties of the people of this age – particularly those of the poor or in any way afflected – these are the joys and hopes, griefs and anxieties of the followers of Christ.' (*Gaudium et Spes*, No 1). It is easy to be an uninvolved observer of the massive 'grief and anxiety' of millions if one sits comfortably in a position of wealth or power. In other words, were one 'stands' often depends on where one 'sits.'

*A Peacemaking Faith*

Technology finds it useful to deal with units divided from one another, and to combine them only when it is useful, and this has some very good results. But it is also subversive and disintegrative of people and groups. Families, neighbourhoods and nations have constant communication problems among themselves today. Polarisation is now a familiar word to many people, as individualism and sectarianism grow, despite generous efforts by some to stop them.

Even before the modern era we had sectionalised people and people's experience into matter and spirit, body and soul, prayer and action, solitude and community, rather than emphasise their basic unity and constant interaction. The distinctiveness of women and men was overemphasised too, not to mention the falling apart of the Christian churches as well as their common stance against other faiths.

Unity and reconciliation are always God's will, as it was from the beginning: 'He (Christ) exists before all things and in him all things hold together ... because God wanted all fullness to be found in him, and through him to reconcile all things to him, everything in heaven and everything on earth, by making peace through his death on the cross.' (Col 1:17,19,20)

We have been offered reconciliation by God in Christ, and God calls us to do the same towards and among others: 'God was in Christ, reconciling the world to himself, not holding men's faults against them, and he has entrusted to us the news that they are reconciled. So we are ambassadors for Christ; it is as though God were appealing through us, and the appeal that we make in Christ's name is: be reconciled to God.' (2 Cor 5:19-20)

Any action which brings people closer together – one to one, families, groups, men and women, marginalised minorities, Christian churches among themselves or with others – is a contribution in faith to building the world as God willed it from the beginning: 'Blessed are the peace makers, they shall be recognised as God's children.' (Mt 5:8)

Notice that it is peace *makers*, not just peace *seekers* nor peace *keepers* whom Jesus called blessed. Peacemaking is a very active and selfless stance; it always implies doing something to bring others together.

*A Disciplined Faith*

Technology often lessens the need for human effort and can thereby provide more time for the use of our higher faculties in a creative way. It facilitates and makes easier, but it also encourages laziness and lack of any effort. It favours 'no' to struggle and 'yes' to surrender.

> Technology favours 'no' to struggle and 'yes' to surrender.

Modernity has provided some of us more easily with more of the essentials, the useful as well as the luxurious. More food but also more junk food is available; golf buggies and cars can put walking out of fashion and make us forget the 'use it or lose it' programme built into every muscle of our *bodies.* Food can go only into fat if it does not go into energy from exercise and so the beautiful God-given mechanism and symmetry of our bodies can become seized-up and shapeless.

This Word of God, written about 200 years before Christ, says: 'Better be poor if healthy and fit, than rich if tormented in body. Health and strength are better than any gold, a robust body than untold wealth.' (Sir 30:14-15)

Modernity maximises the choice or decision to have health and fitness or their opposites. In the New Testament we are given the deeper reason for caring for our body: 'Do you not realise that your body is the temple of the Holy Spirit, who is in you and whom you received from God? ... so use your body for the glory of God.' (1 Cor 6:19-20)

The video industry and the aggressiveness of modern advertising are examples of where technology is used to overemphasise and strain our *emotions*; people say they are 'emotionally drained.' Certainly, the same technology can help us exercise our emotions healthily with well-recorded music or by travelling for a holiday in the mountains. Without discipline, our emotions can become over- or under-stimulated and then either atrophied or exhausted. A well-developed emotional and physical life is more than a mere material achievement; it is part of true spiritual growth.

Our *minds also* can find growthful, useful or enjoyable information more easily today, because of technology. As with our bodies and emotions, it is part of modern spirituality to keep our minds fit, flexible, stimulated and disciplined. This is more difficult than it was for our parents. St Paul warns us to be careful about the temptation to 'follow one craze after another.' (2 Tim 3:6b) and advises us: 'Turn away from godless philosophical discussions and the contradictions of the 'knowledge' which is not knowledge at all; by adopting this, some have missed the goal of faith.' (1 Tim 6:20)

Modernity is becoming a culture which creates its own demands today. One of those is the demand for discipline in our devotional lives. Time for exercises of devotion is not easily found today; it has to be made by choice and decision. The modern person has to create his or her own very personal islands for relaxation with God, for reflection on the ways of God and to thank God for the gifts that have been given to him or her.

This is the age of the half read page,
the quick hash and the mad dash,
the bright night with the nerves tight,
the plane hop, with the brief stop,
the lamp tan, in a short span,
the big shot in a soft spot,
the brain strain and the heart pain,
the cat naps, till the spring snaps
and the fun's done. (R.Blagden)

If that is a fair description of modern life, then Paul's disciplined approach is surely called for in all areas of our lives today: 'All the runners at the stadium are trying to win, but only one of them gets the prize. You must run the same way, meaning to win. All the fighters at the games go into strict training; they do this just to win a wreath that will wither away, but we do it for a wreath that will never wither. That is how I run, intent on winning; that is how I fight, not beating the air. I treat my body hard and make it obey me, for, having been an announcer myself, I should not want to be disqualified.' (1 Cor 9:24-27)

At some time, individuals must find time to consider the price of undisciplined living and the toll of exhaustion on the Spirit. Some things are just not worth it!

Finally let us recall that among the gifts of the Holy Spirit are 'gentleness' and 'self control.' (Gal 5:22b) Today, with technology catering to instinct and instancy, these gifts are more essential than ever in our lives.

### *A Witnessing Faith*

Christians have always accepted the importance of giving 'good' and avoiding 'bad example.' For most it meant behaving virtuously with the hope that others would be encouraged to do the same. 'He said to his disciples, causes of falling are sure to come, but alas for the one through whom they occur! It would be better for him to be thrown into the sea with a millstone round the neck than to be the downfall of a single one of these little ones. Keep watch on yourselves!' (Lk 17:1-3)

The modern world needs more than this, because technology, in its moral neutrality and its mindlessness, has moved many people to an experience of meaninglessness, without deep reasons to live or even to die. As people who have meaning in life through our faith, we have the privilege and obligation to manifest it with quiet enthusiasm and to accompany others in their search for meaning when they seek it. We have good news and we should share it: 'Go out to the whole world; proclaim the Good News to all creation,' (Mk 16:15) is Jesus's word to each of us.

It is not a matter of pushing the Gospel at people but of offering them friendship and service, when and in the way they need it, but unconditionally. Only then, and if they really want it, should we explicitly mention God in whatever way is appropriate for the situation. Friendship and practical kindness are in themselves a proclamation of the Good News; another's readiness for more is God's moment, not ours.

The modern person's high self-awareness and sensitivity about authority, will be most helped when we practice the advice of St Paul: 'Have a profound respect for each other.' (Rom 12:10) Only then can we speak together of God.

People's moral confusion can be helped too as St Peter tells us: 'Always behave honourably among the pagans, so that they can see for themselves what moral lives you lead.' (1 Pet 2:12)

Giving example or witness at a cost to ourselves is part of living our faith: 'Blessed are those who are persecuted in the cause of uprightness: the kingdom of Heaven is theirs.' (Mt 5:10)

*Refused Faith – Sin*

One of the tragedies of the modern world is that it has sin without having a name for it. With the modern person's heightened self-awareness and growing expectations, St Thomas Aquinas helps by reminding us that 'we do not offend God unless we harm ourselves.' (S.C.G. 3:122) God, the creative lover, created us 'in his own image and likeness' to be creative lovers in our turn. This love 'has been poured into our hearts by the Holy Spirit.' (Rom 5:5) We harm ourselves when we fail to believe this and to act on it; we sin.

The source and centre of sin is refusal to believe in

God's love: 'I will send him (the Holy Spirit) to you and when he comes, he will show the world how wrong it was about sin ... in that they refuse to believe in me,' (Jn 16: 7,8,9) and 'No one who remains in him (God) sins and whoever sins has neither seen him nor recognised him.' (1 Jn 3:6)

Many of us have usefully examined our consciences often with a list of sins and we can still do so. But it will also help if we are willing to go more deeply, to ask such questions as:

Am I 'poor in spirit'? i.e. totally dependent on God?
Do I 'hunger and thirst for justice'?
Have I a 'pure heart' in order to receive the mystery of God? (Mt 5:3,6,8) i.e. deeply honest with myself.
Do I really believe, or how deeply am I willing to believe that God loves me unconditionally?

Regarding others near me:

Am I 'gentle...merciful' and a 'peacemaker'? (Mt 5:4,7,9)
How deeply do I live the 'new commandment' of Jesus? 'You must love one another just as I have loved you.' (Jn 13:34)
Do I approach others 'so that they may have life and have it to the full' (Jn 10:10) – the life which God continually gives me?

Mohandas Gandhi listed the sins of the modern world and he helps us to look at our wider sins today:

Wealth without work
pleasure without conscience
knowledge without character
trade without morality
science without humility
worship without sacrifice
politics without principle.

Although all sin is basically personal, there are 'structures of sin' in every society. These are traditions, laws or customs which help the rich and powerful to become richer and more powerful at the expense of the poor and the weak. We are responsible for having these structures removed, and we may even sinfully contribute to them by refusing to act against them.

The Book of Wisdom gives us the basic reason why the modern person seems so often bent on self-harm by misusing the gifts of technology: 'But wretched are they, with their hopes set on dead things, who have given the title of gods to human artifacts, gold or silver skillfully worked.' (Wis 64:10)

## Reviewing Chapter Thirteen

Was there anything in this chapter to which you could immediately relate from your own experience?
Were there any new ideas which you found puzzling or worrisome?
Did you find in this chapter anything of benefit to you in your particular role as a Christian?
*You may find it helpful to make a note of any thoughts from this chapter which you would like to remember.*

## Questions for discussion in your group

1. Faith must be 'deeply owned' today. Why?
2. How do you develop an internalised faith today?
3. Can you find time to ponder and reflect on the events of your day from the standpoint of your deeper values?
4. Re-read the poem on page 105. Is it a fair description of modern life? Do you want to add anything to it or to revise it?
5. Why is the prayer of reflection so important today?
6. Do you ever read the Bible for inspiration?
7. Do you personally find support and solidarity in the Christian community?
8. Where has sin gone to?

# Chapter 14: In Christ and his church

We have seen that our believing today has to be deeply personal, but this does not mean believing just what one chooses. Individualism and subjectivity are encouraged by modern life but faith, like all meaning, needs a Symbol (the Latin word for a creed). Faith has content as well as personal experience and conscience. The church gives us the content (a creed) so that we can have 'one Lord, one faith' (Eph 4:5,6) until the end of time.

A united church is always a special sign of God's presence in the world: 'It is by your love for one another that everyone will recognise you as my disciples.' (Jn 13:35)

This becomes a reality as we live, love, struggle, support one another, celebrate and build God's kingdom of 'saving justice, peace and joy' (Rom 14:17) in the world today. A divided church is a scandal about which we should do whatever we can. God is more worshipped in the prayer of a united community anytime. 'Brothers, we wish you happiness; try to grow perfect; help one another. Be united; live in peace, and the God of love and peace will be with you.' (2 Cor 13:11)

Our faith is not primarily in the church; it is in God and, for those who are called, it is in Jesus Christ. He is the way for our eyes to see and our feet to follow; the truth for our ears to hear and our minds to hold; the life that we may live because he is the vine of which we are the branches (cf. Jn 15) and because he assured us: 'I have loved you just as the Father has loved me,' and asked us, 'Remain in my love.' (Jn 15:9)

Through its teaching authority and its sacramental system, the church has the power and mission to deepen these mysteries in our hearts because it is: 'the church of the living God which upholds the truth and keeps it safe.' (1 Tim 3:15) From all the spiritual books and letters written over centuries and available at the time, the church, under

God's guidance, chose seventy-two of them as God's word; this is the Bible which is thus the result of the church's teaching authority 'to uphold the truth and keep it safe'. Its interpretation of the Bible is similarly guided by God.

'The church, in the light of the Word of God, celebrates the mystery of Christ for the salvation of the world. In reality, the church, the mystical body of Christ, is at the service of the world; it does not desire to do anything other than to serve, to promote the integral development of the human person.' (Pope John Paul II to the Synod, 1985)

*Pilgrims in Hope*

Modernity means constant motion around us and within us; it has made us all spiritual nomads, even refugees. This could be a grace continually calling us away from our favourite – and partly idolatrous – image of God, to find an aspect of faith which perhaps we had lost – its essential quality of evolving and of transition so that we continue to let go of, to search for and discover God anew. Like Abraham, 'our father in faith' who, 'set out not knowing where he was going' (Heb 11:8b), God may be calling us into 'a corporate dark night of the soul', so that we can desire God in trusting love as pilgrims once again, sustained only by the promises of Jesus: 'I will not leave you orphans.' (Jn 14:18) 'Peace I bequeath to you, my own peace I give you.' (v.27) 'Do not let your hearts be troubled or afraid.' (v.27) 'And look, I am with you always; yes, to the end of time.' (Mt 16:20)

These simple texts hold a deep religious truth for believers in their efforts to live with constant change, much ambiguity and no small anxiety today.

Faith has always been linked to hope and this virtue needs to be emphasised today when pessimism pervades much of the news: 'And this hope will not let us down, because the love of God has been poured into hearts by the Holy Spirit which has been given us.' (Rom 5:5)

Nor is it a matter of hope for the hereafter; there is hope in the modern world. In Part One, we quoted the opinion of Pope John Paul II in 1979. Here is his more hopeful assessment ten years later: 'Our own century has experienced such terrible wars and political tensions, such offenses against life and freedom, such seemingly intractable sources of suffering – including the present-day tragedies of the international drug trade and the increasing spread of AIDS – that some people may hesitate to express too much hope or to be over optimistic about the future. Yet many will agree that the world is living through a *moment of extraordinary awakening*. The old problems remain and new ones arise; but there is also a growing awareness of an opportunity being offered to give birth to a new and better era; a time to involve one another in frank and truthful collaboration in order to meet the great challenges facing humanity at the end of the twentieth century. The opportunity I speak of is not something clearly definable. It is more like the confluence of many complex global developments in the fields of science and technology, in the economic world, in a growing political maturity of peoples and in the formation of public opinion. Perhaps it is right to say that what we are experiencing is a change, however slow and fragile, in the direction of the worlds' concerns, and an increasing, if sometimes grudging willingness to accept the implications of planetary interdependence from which no one can truly escape.'

(Copenhagen 7.6.89)